WALT DISNEY
STUDIO
COFFEE SHOP

BURBANK, CALIFORNIA

EAT LIKE WALT

The Wonderful World of Disney Food

Marcy Carriker Smothers

Foreword by
John Lasseter

Afterword by
Tom Fitzgerald

EDITIONS

LOS ANGELES • NEW YORK

CONTENTS

DEDICATION

FOR WALT DISNEY

As a child, going to Disneyland was always my favorite day of the year. I'd arrive giddy with excitement, never wanting the day to end. When the park closed, I was exhausted, falling asleep in my grandfather's arms on the way to the tram. Pirates of the Caribbean, my favorite attraction, was always our first ride—a tradition I maintain today. We were allowed one special treat: mine was chocolate fudge from the Candy Palace, but the highlight was the Main Street Electrical Parade. What is this feeling? The same feeling I have as an adult each and every time I enter the gate, see the train station and giant floral Mickey in front of me, pass under the railroad tunnel into Town Square, and get my first glimpse of Main Street, U.S.A.? The feeling I share with millions and millions of people at the Happiest Place on Earth? Whatever the magic is, Disneyland is my land. It's my source of joy and inspiration.

Thanks, Walt.

John Lasseter

FOREWORD

I grew up in Whittier, California, about a half hour drive from Anaheim. My family went to Disneyland at least once a year, and that was always my favorite day of the year, because Disneyland was my favorite place on earth. My memories of those trips are filled with rides, parades, and meetings with characters, but they are also full of food experiences. Food always tasted better at Disneyland—the hamburgers, the hot dogs, even the popcorn made by those tiny people turning the wheels of the poppers. The pinnacle, of course, was the Blue Bayou. For most of my childhood, I was convinced that the Blue Bayou was the single greatest eating experience on the planet. Sitting under the lanterns, watching the fireflies flicker as the boats for Pirates of the Caribbean passed by, eating my delicious Monte Cristo sandwich, I was just transported. It was such a magical experience, I didn't want the moment to ever end.

My good friend, food and wine expert Marcy Smothers, is just as much of a Disneyland fanatic as I am. When she came up with the idea for a culinary history of Disneyland, I was immediately excited—what a unique perspective! It was a fresh way of looking at Disney history, but one that any fan would instantly be able to relate to. Because she and I are neighbors up in Northern California and share a geeky interest in research, I checked in with her regularly to hear about her latest historical finds. She soon told me that she had realized you can't really tell the food history of Disneyland without looking at the food history of Walt Disney himself, and the food history of the Walt Disney Studios.

As she said it, my brain started lighting up with my own memories. I worked at the Walt Disney Studios in the summer of 1975, just nine years after Walt passed away. The studio then—and even later when I worked there as an animator from 1979 to 1984—still looked and operated almost exactly as it had when Walt was alive. I vividly remembered eating at the studio commissary. My favorite thing to order was always the chili (I discovered later that that had been Walt's favorite as well), with a slice of custard pie for dessert. I never knew that you could combine custard and a pie together, but it was the best! The Tea Lounge on the second floor of the Ink and Paint building served amazing buttermilk tea cakes in the mornings and milkshakes in the afternoons. On a few occasions I even had lunch in the Coral Room and the Penthouse, as a guest of the veteran artists I was getting to know that summer.

Before that conversation with Marcy, I had never thought about the food at the studio at any length. But her observation got me thinking about my memories in a new way. I realized that Walt, who had put so much thought into the Blue Bayou, was the same person who had planned out the restaurants at the studio. (In fact, the Monte Cristo sandwich was on the commissary's menu before it became famous at the Blue Bayou!)

Eat Like Walt: The Wonderful World of Disney Food gives you a great sense of Walt Disney's creative journey in designing Disneyland as an immersive experience, in thinking about food as an important part of creating something enjoyable and memorable. It's a fascinating story, connecting the personal, professional, and public sides of Walt Disney's life: from his simple tastes and down-to-earth home life, to his attention to detail and good quality in everything he touched, to his incredible understanding of storytelling and entertainment as a complete experience.

As someone who was lucky enough to have experienced many of the things described in this book firsthand, I loved getting to revisit those memories and learning more about people and places I knew only in name before this. Marcy paints an in-depth picture of the food at the Disney Studios and Disneyland during Walt's lifetime. Reading it, you can imagine what these places were like when they first opened—what it must have been like to see Walt standing in line at the commissary for his lunch, or seated at a back table at the Carnation Café. Any Disney fan knows how exciting it is to get to hear a new part of the Disney story. This one is a special treat.

—JOHN LASSETER

DISNEYLAND: WHERE THE FOOD IS AS FABULOUS AS THE FUN

He was never happier than the Opening Day of Disneyland.
—Diane Disney Miller

In 1955 the United States entered the Vietnam conflict. Rosa Parks refused to give up her seat on a Montgomery, Alabama, bus. McDonald's served its first hamburger. Joe DiMaggio was inducted into the Baseball Hall of Fame. Anaheim, California, had a population of 30,081 people. Oh, and Disneyland opened.

The typical American postwar repast was bland and boring. Meats were boiled and vegetables were often overcooked. Julia Child had yet to publish *Mastering the Art of French Cooking*, which would change the way American housewives cooked at home.

Yet almost two decades before the California food revolution, Walt Disney was planning a revolution of his own. He knew that food could be more than nourishment—it could be entertaining, too. The concept of families eating and playing at the same time was an innovation in mid-century America. Food in Disneyland wasn't gray or humdrum. It was full of fantasy and color!

When the Magic Kingdom opened its gates to a preview audience on July 17, 1955, Walt declared that the twenty eateries spread throughout the park were attractions unto themselves: "Like Adventureland and Fantasyland, the new 'Kingdom of Good Eating' at Disneyland is another great attraction. Fine restaurants, unique refreshment stands, and interesting luncheon spots abound in Disneyland. Dining Disneyland-style is an unforgettable experience. The food's as fabulous as the fun, too."

Producing fond food memories was a priority from day one. The October 10, 1955 *Disneyland News* promised Guests, "Your meal at Disneyland will be one of your more pleasant memories, no matter what spot you choose for lunch, dinner, or just a snack. This is due to both the ingenuity of Disneyland's designers and the rigid high-quality standards required of lessees who operate food service concessions."

Forty-seven lessees signed contracts with Walt Disney Productions, the majority of them five-year terms, with the clever condition that the first and last year be paid in advance. It was their commitment, along with sponsors, that helped finance the park. The lessees' requirements to be "Disneyland Style" were the same for fine dining and fast food: it was all part of the show.

Reputable companies (and their products) like the Coca-Cola Company, Sunkist, Frito-Lay (Fritos), Maxwell House, and Quaker Oats (Aunt Jemima) set up shop on Main Street, U.S.A. and throughout the other four lands.

Some were ready for Guests and had their venues operating on July 17, 1955, including the Carnation Ice Cream Parlor, Swift's Red Wagon Inn, and The Golden Horseshoe. Others opened in the following weeks, such as the Chicken of the Sea Pirate Ship and Restaurant, which was only half finished on Opening Day.

Nearly four million meals were served during Disneyland's first year. Capacity was planned for eight thousand Guests an hour, which proved to be inadequate when the crowds swelled.

On Opening Day, the lines for food were long, not just for takeaway food and snacks, but for fine dining as well. Three thousand Guests waited for a table at the elegant Red Wagon Inn. Disneyland's records waggishly reflect that early in the afternoon, the doorman said, "Right this way, please . . . the hostess will show you to your seats." But toward the end of the hectic day the doorman's greeting changed to, "Right this way, please . . . the hostess will show you to your *sheets*."

Prices ranged from thirty-five cents for a hamburger to three dollars and fifty cents for a prime rib dinner with all the fixings. Coffee was taken seriously at the park. From the start, Walt was emphatic that coffee was "only worth a dime."

Card Walker, vice president of advertising and sales, further insisted, "Disneyland will always have a ten-cent cup of coffee." It wasn't until well after Walt's passing in 1966 that the price increased.

Innovation was not just for the attractions; it applied to the restaurants, too. The publicity team referred to it as, "Thematic Feeding: a program where the food served, either by the character of the food itself, or by the method of service, is themed to the area."

Tomorrowland, which from Opening Day was looking ahead to the food service procedures of the future, utilized automated vending machines to match its futuristic theme. New Orleans Square's Blue Bayou—with its Cajun- and Creole-themed cuisines, served in a setting that evokes a feeling of being under eternal moonlight on a Southern mansion's terrace—opened in 1967 and is considered the pioneer of themed-dining experiences.

Just as a meal is much more than what's presented on the plate, the culinary history of Disneyland is much more than the food served in the park. Through the looking glass of Disneyland's culinary history, we can learn about Walt's vision for each and every Guest who entered the park's gates.

Eat Like Walt is also a peek inside Walt's personal life at home and at work—how he ate and what he ate. For such a remarkable man, whose life was exciting and multifaceted, his food preferences were quite basic and, daresay, *boring* (by today's standards). His daughter Diane Disney Miller noted that it stemmed from his early, more meager meals. "Before he married Mother, Father had eaten in hash houses and [at] lunch wagons for so many years [in order to save money] that he developed a hash house/lunch wagon appetite."

When it came to eating, Walt was more of an everyman than a pampered celebrity. As songwriter and Disney Legend Richard Sherman summarized, "Walt didn't like fancy stuff . . . he was a very complex man, but his tastes were very simple."

These culinary leanings could be seen in some of Disney's early movies. Mickey Mouse's first words—*ever*—were "hot dogs, hot dogs," voiced by Walt himself in 1929's *The Karnival Kid*. Hot dogs were one of Walt's favorite foods. He liked them plain and he liked them often. Thus, he insisted that hot dog stands be sprinkled throughout the park, and in Disneyland's first year 935,460 hot dogs were sold. (By the way, the oft quoted "a wienie on every corner" did not refer to frankfurters; it's a term for a visual design element that draws attention, such as the park's Sleeping Beauty Castle.)

Hot dogs figure into the park's sanitation concerns, too. Walt reportedly paced off the distance between trash cans based on how long it took to eat a hot dog; he wanted to be sure there would be no reason to drop wrappers on the ground. He also helped design the trash cans, theming them to blend in seamlessly with each land and implementing the swinging doors on them so Guests wouldn't have to lift the lid or see the trash inside.

The disposal of that garbage was one of the myriad details Walt personally attended to as well. To handle that job, he instructed Chuck Boyajian, the first manager of custodial relations, to go to a "top-notch" hotel and sit in the lobby for a weekend and observe. Boyajian's task was to note how a first-class operation handled garbage, while making the effort as invisible to Guests as possible. (Walt was determined to keep Disneyland spotless, even if that meant picking up trash himself—but also to satisfy Lillian: "When I started on Disneyland my wife used to say, 'But why do you want to build an amusement park? They're so dirty.' I told her that was just the point—mine wouldn't be.")

Culinary interests were perhaps not always foremost on

Walt's agenda. But even in 1934—nearly four years before his first feature film, *Snow White and the Seven Dwarfs*, would be released, and six years before the Walt Disney Studios would begin operating in Burbank (and over twenty years before Disneyland opened)—Walt was famous enough to be asked to contribute a recipe that would be published in *Better Homes and Gardens* magazine. (Sales of nearly five million box office tickets tied to Mickey Mouse shorts and films had made Walt a well-known figure.) *Macaroni Mickey Mousse* may be the first recipe attributed to Walt. (The double s in *Mousse* is not a typo, although it is a perfect pun.) A mousse can be a pudding or something that's molded, such as Walt's macaroni and cheese casserole.

According to the text accompanying the recipe, Walt's hand-feeding of mice, and an affinity for one particularly friendly one, became the inspiration for Mickey Mouse. "It all goes back to my cartooning days in Kansas City [Missouri]. I had a wastebasket, and mice would get in there to find scraps of food we'd sometimes throw there.

"I put them in boxes and fed them," Walt further noted. "One of them got so tame he made a playground of a little cleat along the top of my drawing board. He'd run back and forth on that shelf, while I was at work, and I became very much attached to him. I called him Mortimer at first, but changed it to Mickey. That's how it all started."

While Walt was an animal lover, and would not allow any pests to be exterminated on his property, this tale and those similar to it appear to be myth. "Stories have been printed about how Walt got interested in mice back on the farm in Marceline, Missouri, when he was a kid," Lillian Disney stated categorically to *McCall's* magazine in 1953. "Newspaper articles have told how Walt used to have a pet mouse named Mickey, which lived in his wastebasket during the freelance cartoon days in Kansas City . . . but when he created Mickey Mouse there was no symbolism or background for the idea. He simply thought the mouse would make a cute character to animate."

From little details, like the peanuts that fueled Walt's dream to create a permanent playground for family fun, "the idea for Disneyland came about when my daughters were very young and Saturday was always Daddy's day with the two daughters," he later recounted. "I'd sit while they rode the merry-go-round and . . . sit on a bench, you know, eating peanuts—and I felt that there should be something built where the parents and the children could have fun together." To big ideas, such as building four restaurants at his state-of-the-art studio in Burbank, there is a lot to learn about Walt Disney—the public and the private person—through the wide and intimate lens of food.

In the years since Disneyland opened, the food landscape has changed a lot, and yet only a little at the same time. Many restaurants have been replaced or re-themed, keeping pace with America's emerging cuisine trends, yet the spirit of the dining experience is largely untouched.

So, just as there's a story for every attraction at Disneyland, there is a story for many menu items as well. Sometimes it's obvious, like gumbo in New Orleans Square. Other times it's subtle, like the tiny land-themed puppets that turn the drums on popcorn carts throughout the park. (Even though Disneyland's popcorn is flavored with coconut oil, Walt liked his elsewhere with extra butter.)

Disneyland's food (and the presentation of it) transports us as much as it satiates us.

Food is fun! And it's a huge part of the Disneyland experience. Sit back, relax, and enjoy the ride on this culinary tour of the Happiest Place on Earth.

Good Eating Land at Disneyland!

Like Adventureland and Fantasyland, the new "Kingdom of Good Eating" at Disneyland is another great attraction. Fine restaurants, unique refreshment stands and interesting luncheon spots abound in Disneyland. Dining Disneyland style is an unforgettable experience. The food's as fabulous as the fun, too!

In all Disneyland only Swift's Premium Meats, Swift's Poultry and other Swift's fine foods will be served—exclusively

The Red Wagon Inn is one of several charming eating places in Disneyland. It is resplendent in the elegance of a by-gone era reminiscent of the most famed eating houses of yesterday. All appointments are authentic mementos of the gay and glamorous 90's—including the stained glass ceiling, entrance hall and foyer taken from the St. James home in Los Angeles, one of the West's most noted old mansions. Atmosphere, however, is not confined to the building alone. The menu itself brings back visions of historic good eating—featuring steaks and chops.

The Swift Wagon—horse-drawn replica of the 1890's that services all eating establishments in Disneyland with Swift fine foods.

Grandmother shopped in a store like Swift's Market House on Disneyland's Main Street. Here we find the old-fashioned butcher in straw hat and cuffs, the pot-bellied stove and shelves lined with authentic old-time meat and grocery products. Swift & Company, whose quality meats are served exclusively in Disneyland, is the sponsor of this exhibit.

Swift

The Chicken Plantation at Disneyland is a gay antebellum river plantation house, reproduced in every nostalgic detail. French provincial decor and old Southern Hospitality make the Chicken Plantation a memorable spot. You'll want to visit The Plantation soon.

Chapter 1
WALT AT HOME

I have one comforting thought. Food isn't that important to Walt.
—LILLIAN DISNEY

He had a simple palate.
—DIANE DISNEY MILLER

He ate like a human being.
—RON MILLER

Walt was fifteen when he had his first steady job as a "news butcher" on a Chicago–Kansas City train. He sold concessions—fruit, candy, papers, and magazines—acknowledging that he used most of his meager profits for food. Soon thereafter, Walt worked in a jelly factory He recounted: "I nailed up boxes, and I'd run the bottle washer. And then I used to mash the apples to make pectin. You see for jelly, I did anything."

In 1918, not yet seventeen, Walt was eager to join the postwar effort. Too young to join the army, he enlisted in the Red Cross Ambulance Corps, forging the paperwork for his passport. When he returned from France eleven months later, and much to his father's chagrin, he did not want to resume his job at the jelly factory. He joined his brother Roy in Kansas City instead, where he interviewed for a job as an apprentice in an art shop. "I went up to see these guys, two fellows by the name of Pesmen and Rubin. They had the art for Gray Advertising Company. I went up there with these samples, and they were all these corny things I had done in France. Well, by gosh, they hired me."

From humble beginnings to becoming one of the most famous men on the planet, Walt never became a foodie nor an adventurous eater. Eating was not a priority.

In the early Hollywood days, Walt lived with his brother in a tiny apartment; Roy handled the cooking duties. Lillian recounted in an interview with *McCall's* magazine in 1953, "I've always teased Walt that he asked me to marry him so soon after Roy married Edna Francis, a Kansas City girl, because he needed someone to fix his meals."

Edna occasionally invited bachelor Walt to dinner while Roy was recuperating in a veteran's hospital. "But Walt would get involved in working out some idea and forget to turn up until ten or eleven at night. Once, soon after we were married,

Walt did the same thing to me. When it came to dinnertime he wandered out of the studio to the corner beanery for a bowl of soup and then right back to the studio to continue with his idea. It wasn't until far into the night that he woke up to the fact he had a bride at home who had cooked a dinner and was waiting to throw it in his face when he turned up," recounted Lillian, before adding, "However, I forgave him. You can't stay mad at Walt for very long."

Walt ate very plainly, according to his wife. "He liked basic foods. He *loved* chili."

Indeed, the two were inseparable. Walt liked to eat chili at the high-toned Beverly Hills restaurant Chasen's, though he was just as happy, or happier, with a combination of Gebhardt's and Dennison's canned chili. Son-in-law Ron Miller muses, "He liked foods he was used to.

"My analysis of the whole chili and beans in cans story," Miller further notes, "[though] he never said this to me, but I have a feeling, [is] just like a lot of young people, they go to France, they go overseas, [and] all of a sudden [it's just] the rich food. I'm used to chili and beans, potatoes and gravy, and steaks. The next time I go to France, I'm going to take my own food and pack a bag."

Walt's granddaughter Jenny Miller Goff adds, "I remember Granny saying that when they would go to Europe in the late 1930s and early 1940s, they would have Vienna sausages. It was just easy. Food wasn't plentiful. They would sit in the hotel room and eat crackers and Vienna sausages."

Domestic travel had its challenges, too. When Walt flew to Pittsburgh to pitch Westinghouse for the 1964–65 World's Fair, he was served a lobster salad in the corporate dining room. On the way back to the hotel, Walt turned to his team and said, "Boy, that wasn't a very good lunch. Let's get a cheeseburger and a chocolate shake."

Walt had as much fun with the family's soda fountain as his daughters. According to Diane, "He made a mean chocolate ice-cream soda." He also liked to make concoctions he knew no guest would want to eat. Imagineer and Disney Legend Bob Gurr recalls, "He was a tease. Walt would say, 'Here, I am going to make you something special' and he knew no one would refuse him."

Indeed, one of the most endearing and lesser-known qualities about Walt's personality was how much he liked to kid around. A few weeks before daughter Diane's wedding to Ron, a USC football player she met on a blind date, Walt was watching a game with his soon to be son-in-law. Ron was dressed casually in shorts, and when Diane entered the room wearing jeans, Walt said wryly, "Are you two going to get married dressed like that?" On the day of their nuptials, Walt carried the joke further. As told by Diane: "Once a gag-man, always a gagman. Dad surprised us with some unusual bride-and-groom figures on the top of our wedding cake." The humorous cake topper had Diane dressed in Levi's, with Ron barefoot in Bermuda shorts and carrying a football helmet.

According to Diane's narration in the Walt Disney Family Museum, "Over the years, we had a succession of cooks in the kitchen. Our last one in the Woking Way house . . . was Bessie Postalwaite, a good cook, an intelligent woman, and a Missourian. That fact established a special bond between her and Dad. She knew how to prepare food that he liked to eat—really good hash made from the previous night's roast beef, bread pudding, apple brown Betty, chicken potpie (with biscuits on top), fried chicken, broiled chicken, and chicken-fried steak. When tomatoes were in season, she'd bring him a little side dish of them with vinegar and sugar." When the Disney family moved to their Holmby Hills home, Bessie retired. And a new cook blew in. . . .

Thelma Pearl Howard arrived in 1951—and stayed thirty years. Christopher, Walt and Lillian's first grandchild, struggled to pronounce her name and thus she was affectionately dubbed "Fou Fou."

The Disney grandchildren grew up in Fou Fou's kitchen. "I don't know how she did it. All of us were sprawled in her kitchen drawing pictures. She was always in a good mood. She loved us and never made us feel as if we were in her way," recalls Jenny. "Thanksgivings with her were the best. She would wrap the turkey in a towel, swaddling it like a baby in a blanket, then walk around the kitchen saying 'Poor little turkey.'"

Then just like Mary Poppins—Walt often referred to Thelma as such—snap! The job became a game. "We would pluck the quills that were left on the bird, taking turns; this was before pre-cleaned supermarket turkeys, and it was so much fun," Jenny says.

Always by her side was another of Walt's granddaughters, Tamara Miller, who describes Fou Fou's kitchen as a sanctuary. "It was all about food, but it was also a clubhouse. That's where we stayed, that's where we hung out. There was this huge island in the middle of the kitchen and we were always playing up there."

Diane was equally besotted with Thelma. "She would be in full command—giving orders [to the children], moving quickly, laughing right along with them. Living the dream."

Son-in-law Ron reminisces affectionately, "She was marvelous. You have to really respect this woman because what they [Walt and Lillian] had in Holmby Hills wasn't a huge home, but it was a relatively big home. She did everything. And she insisted on doing everything. She cleaned every room, she vacuumed, she took care of the grandkids, and she made every meal."

WALT DISNEYS FAVORITES —

CHICKEN FRY CUBE STAKE

ROAST LAMB — POTATOES + GRAVY

PAN FRIED CHICKEN WITH
POTATOES + GRAVY

ROAST CHICKEN WITH
DRESSING + GRAVY

SPAM + EGGS WITH
BISCUITS + HONEY

OYSTER STEW WITH
CRACKERS + CHEESE

BREADED VEAL CUTTLETS
BREAD + GRAVY

CHASONS CHILLI + BEANS

NOTE → ONLY ONE VEGETABLE
WITH MEALS — CORN —
CANNED PEAS — LEAF SPINNACH
STEWED TOMATOES — ETC.

SALADS —

CARROT + RAISANS?

WALDORF — x

TOMATOES + CUCUMBER

CHEFS SALAD —

DESSERTS —

JELLO — ALL FLAVORS
WITH PIECES OF FRUIT —

DIET CUSTARDS —

PINAPLE — FRESH OR
CANNED

FRUIT — FRESH OR
CANNED —

HomeMade Soups?

Fou Fou was a passionate sports fan, delighting in one-dollar wagers with Ron. She pored over *Star* magazine and the *National Enquirer*. "Here she is with Frank Sinatra living across the street and Gregory Peck next door; she's working for Walt Disney, for goodness' sakes, and she's reading about the celebrities in her neighborhood," giggles Jenny.

Fou Fou was a perfectionist, cooking everything from scratch, never using anything canned or frozen. "Her apple pie was the best in the world. Grandpa liked his with cheddar cheese on it," says Jenny.

She made what the grandkids called "dog biscuits" using the scraps from the crust. Tamara remembers, "She rolled out the leftover dough, lathered it in butter, then added cinnamon

{ABOVE} *This is the only photograph the Disney family has of Fou Fou. It's enshrined at The Walt Disney Family Museum in San Francisco.*

and sugar. Then she'd roll it up, cut it, put the slices on a round pan with the sides touching each other, and bake them. They were really good!"

It wasn't unusual for Walt and Lillian to eat dinner on trays in front of the television; however, when family was coming over, a typical meal at the Disney home might start with a platter of salami, yellow cheese, crackers, and black olives. Deviled eggs, reserved for special occasions, weren't fancy. Fou Fou prepared them with mayonnaise, mustard, and salt and pepper, then dusted with her version of pixie dust—paprika. "That paprika was magical in the mashed potatoes, too," says Tamara. "They were incredible."

If you opened the Disney family's refrigerator, you were likely to see a partitioned glass relish tray holding radishes, scallions, celery, carrots, pickles, and turnips with fresh ice under it no matter what time of the day it was. Small glass bottles of Dr Pepper, 7UP, Orange Crush, and Strawberry Crush were at the ready. Hot dogs and bologna were omnipresent even though Lillian was not amused by Walt's antics. "[He] ruins every suit he owns by coming through the kitchen when he gets home at night and [filling] his pockets with bologna and hot dogs for our nine-year-old French poodle, Dee Dee." The family dog wasn't the only one who liked cold hot dogs—her master did, too.

When Walt tired of Lillian's oft-repeated meals, he composed a list of his dinner dos and don'ts. Presenting it to Fou Fou he said, "Thelma, here's a list of the things I like to eat." She posted it on the refrigerator to use as a reference. On that handwritten list, with his signature loops and humble misspellings (he never graduated high school), were Walt's approved entrees, meat-centric and simply prepared, usually roasted or pan-fried.

Vegetables did not take center stage on Walt's plate. They

were restricted to "only one" and included canned peas, beans, leaf spinach, and stewed tomatoes. The salads could vary and included carrot-raisin salad, Waldorf salad, chef's salad, and tomatoes with cucumbers. Homemade soup was written in the margin as a question, perhaps because he almost preferred canned products (which were considered more than acceptable in mid-century America).

Beverages, like Walt's food, were not elaborate. He liked V8 juice and black coffee. His favorite cocktail was a Scotch mist, a concoction of crushed ice, Scotch—Black & White or Canadian Club—and a twist of lemon. When the grandkids were visiting, there would be a long spoon in his glass with slices of oranges on the rim. "I was so excited to get that orange slice," says Jenny. "We would ask for the ice," adds Tamara.

Desserts were served nightly at home. Walt preferred pies—especially apple, boysenberry, and frozen lemon chiffon pie. He also enjoyed apple brown Betty, bread pudding, baked apples, gingerbread, and red JELL-O with fruit. Butterscotch was Walt's favorite flavor, either as a pudding or Chinese candy cookies, a confection of chow mein noodles, peanuts, and melted butterscotch.

Walt could be very particular with his food. Lillian acknowledged in an interview with Bob Thomas (renowned Associated Press reporter and Walt Disney biographer) that, "Sometimes he could be annoyed by something he was served." She remembered that one evening after Thelma presented Walt with a handmade whipped cream cake, he groused that he didn't like cake. Lillian decided to have some playful revenge. "I got so put out that I picked up a piece of the whipped cream and threw it at him. It hit him right in the face. And he picked up some whipped cream and threw it at me. Then we started throwing it back and forth at each other," she recounted. "I remember that I got some on the wall-

paper. . . . It left a grease mark and I had to change it."

Fou Fou was like family. Several years after she retired, Diane noticed she hadn't received her usual Christmas card. Worried, she found her in a shabby nursing home sharing a ward with men and women. Diane moved Fou Fou to a private room in a retirement community with beautiful gardens. She visited often and sent fresh flowers every Monday. When Fou Fou passed away in 1994 her estate was worth nearly nine million dollars, thanks to regular birthday and Christmas gifts of company stock from Walt. She lived a frugal life and held on to almost every share, save purchasing a modest home, as she perceived selling her stock as being disloyal to her boss.

Fou Fou's hard-earned money went to her developmentally disabled adult son and to establish the Thelma Pearl Howard Foundation benefiting arts-based education enrichment activities for disadvantaged children.

Fou Fou was practically perfect in every way.

Chapter 2
WALT AT THE STUDIO

Enthusiasm and optimism together. He was enthusiastic about everything.
He never thought anything would turn out badly.
—Lillian Disney

alt never set out to be a restaurateur, but he became one. His experiences at each of his successive studios helped him to define what he wanted for his crown jewel—the Walt Disney Studios in Burbank.

In 1921, Walt's fledgling Laugh-O-gram Films studio in Kansas City used a small restaurant, the Forest Inn, as the off-premises commissary. When Walt was struggling, the owners offered him a line of credit, which may have saved him. "It was probably the blackest time of my life," he said later.

Next came the Disney Brothers Cartoon Studio on Kingswell Avenue in Hollywood, first in the back half of a real estate office and later in a store next door. Without a commissary, Walt ate almost every day at a nearby malt shop and lunch counter. In 1926 a new studio, albeit modest, was completed on Hyperion Avenue—the birthplace of Mickey Mouse. Roy referred to it as "bacon and eggs without the bacon." Although this was his third iteration, there still wasn't a commissary on

the premises. Walt and his animators, some of whom eventually became known as the "Nine Old Men," ate lunch often at Tam O'Shanter, a restaurant in the nearby Los Angeles neighborhood of Los Feliz.

Most employees brought their lunch; however, if they were still hungry they might forage for candy bars from Walt's secretary's desk. The other option was a little "shop," more like an alcove, with sundries. Entrepreneurial secretary Mary Flanigan sold sandwiches, soft drinks, candy, and gum to her coworkers, along with cigarettes and aspirin.

Walt's groundbreaking first feature-length animated film, *Snow White and the Seven Dwarfs*, was made at Hyperion, and a restaurant figures heavily into the pitch that led to the production. Animator Ken Anderson tells the tale in *Working with Walt: Interviews with Disney Artists*:

> One night after we had been doing shorts, Walt gave us sixty-five cents for dinner, and the fifty of us in animation went across the street to Ma Applebaum's. I got a dinner—most of us did—for fifty cents and saved the fifteen. Then we came back to the little soundstage. Ward Kimball and I sat next to one another. Walt was in a subdued light on the main floor . . . Walt had this whole thing for his stage. He thought out and dreamed this whole Snow White business. We didn't know that. He spent whatever time we got back from dinner—6:30, 7:00—until nearly midnight acting and not only describing the plot and the picture, but acting out the individual characters and the parts. He lit such a fire under those of us there, that it never occurred to us we were ever going to do anything else in our whole lives except that picture.

{ABOVE} *Walt (wearing the striped shirt) with Mary Flanigan in her Hyperion Avenue sundries shop.*

Snow White and the Seven Dwarfs premiered at Hollywood's Carthay Circle Theatre on December 21, 1937. It won an Honorary Academy Award, along with seven mini statuettes, and defined Walt as a compelling storyteller and innovator of a brand-new art form.

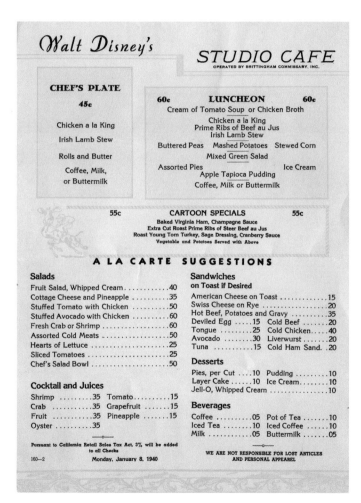

"One of Walt's greatest wishes has always been that his employees could work in ideal surroundings, as the dean of animated cartoons realizes that a happy personnel turns out the best work."
—*Hollywood Reporter*, October 10, 1940

In 1938, while planning his state-of-the-art, Streamline Moderne studio in Burbank, Walt got serious about restaurants. He wanted his employees to have access to quality meals at fair prices, which he subsidized, right on the lot. He also knew that this convenience would increase productivity.

Walt and some of his staff moved into the Walt Disney Studios in January 1940, the same year *Pinocchio* won two Oscars for Best Score and Best Song. Four restaurants were in various stages of construction, with temporary food service at the Studio Cafe on the Live Action Stage (a novelty, since all Walt's movies were animated up until this point). Operated by Brittingham Commissary, the interim facility opened after a hectic weekend of day and night construction to be ready for the first lunch on Monday, January 8. The setting was rather elegant, with a cafeteria and dining room, flowers on every table, and a varied menu with reasonable prices.

Victor Bronnais, well-known in America's restaurant industry for tenures at the Hotel del Coronado in San Diego and Santa Anita racetrack in Arcadia, California, where he oversaw everything from the fancy food to hot dog stands, was appointed restaurants manager. He shared Walt's commitment to quality food and service at good prices.

"The facts are these: Thursday, March 21st, the new studio restaurant opened. Everybody was there. 1,110 meals were served in one day. 73 doz. eggs were used, 56 pies, and 1,350 cups of coffee. There were almost as many 'oh's' and 'ah's' over the food, the color scheme, and the waitresses than were heard when movie audiences first began seeing Dopey on the screen. It was a grand success."
—The Bulletin, March 23, 1940

Walt Disney's Studio Restaurant, as noted in the write-up, opened on March 21, 1940. It was designer-decorated, air-conditioned, and soundproofed. Waitresses attended the tables. (A cafeteria line was added in 1953 when the studio got busier with live-action production.)

Presaging the theming at Disneyland, characters from Walt's movies were the stars of the menu: Snow White's Special, Stromboli's Favorite Sandwich, Monstro's Morsel, and The Little Pig's Salad Bowl. The Monte Cristo sandwich, popular in mid-century Southern California, appeared on the Studio Restaurant's menu and would go on to become iconic at Disneyland when it debuted on the Blue Bayou's menu in 1967. Among the more unusual offerings for a workplace was a selection of beers and imported cheeses.

Writing for *American Magazine* in August 1955, journalist Don Eddy went to the studio to get the answer to one question: "What amazing secret does Disney use to make his own dreams, and yours and mine, come true?" In his article, he describes the first time he saw Walt:

He was waiting stoically in line in his small, crowded studio-cafeteria, sandwiched between typists and stagehands. He looked no different than the man next door—aged fifty-four, average height, average weight, amiable, needed a haircut, his clipped mustache almost invisible against sun-toasted skin, his regulation Hollywood uniform of slacks and sports shirt as casual as though they had been the first things at hand when he got up that morning.

I watched him inch along as the line progressed, take his tray and silverware from the stacks, thoughtfully select a luncheon of orange juice, fruit salad, and chili con carne, wait until the cashier totaled his check—and pay for it! I never before saw a movie producer pay for luncheon in his own restaurant. He carried his loaded tray through the noisy crowd to an unoccupied table, arranged his dishes on the bare boards, stacked his tray on a vacant chair, and signaled the waitress to bring coffee. He had to signal three times; the waitress nodded understandingly each time, but went on with what she was doing. In moviedom, where top producers often had their private dining rooms, I never before saw anything like that. . . .

Walt tended to make lunch at the studio his big meal of the day and then pick at dinner. Diane recalled her mother saying, "Why should Thelma and I plan a meal when all Walt really wants is a can of chili or spaghetti?" Lillian arranged with Walt's secretary to call and report what Walt had for lunch, "because when he didn't like the dinner, he often used the excuse he had it for lunch."

Chili, of course, was omnipresent. Walt ate it several times a week in the Studio Restaurant, always with crackers, and he was prone to stash a few packets in his pocket. As a result, there were crumbs in his suits every time they went to the dry cleaner. "He has excellent taste in clothes, but he won't take care of them," said Lillian.

Victor instituted a pass system so employees could bring guests to lunch and dinner on the lot. Walt invited nonemployees to use the Studio Restaurant, too. He was one of the founders of St. Joseph's Hospital across the street and allowed hospital employees to use the commissary as their own, a practice that was continued until security concerns arose following the 9/11 terror attacks in 2001.

{ABOVE} *The horseshoe counter in the coffee shop.*

COFFEE SHOP
MARCH 1940–1956

The coffee shop was adjacent to the Studio Restaurant, also air-conditioned, and decorated in blue, yellow, and chromium. It featured horseshoe-style counters with sixty-seven attached stools and several tables.

ANIMATION COFFEE SHOP
1940–1941

The Animation Coffee Shop was located on the first floor of the Animation Building. It was unofficially known as Mary Flanigan's after Roy asked the studio's "institution" to run it. The menu offered simple breakfasts such as fruit, sweet rolls, and cereal. Sandwiches and desserts were offered at lunch with an assortment of pies and ice creams for dessert. Some employees ate meals at their desks, prompting this post in the company newsletter:

The Bulletin, February 23, 1940
OUTLET FOR ARTISTIC MUSE WORRIES
MARY FLANIGAN

Good-natured Mary Flanigan has sent a mild complaint to *The Bulletin* to the effect that some of the boys and girls have forgotten to return the silver from the Coffee Shop, and they have been abusing the dishes. She feels that a great many knives, forks[,] and spoons are scattered around the building. Mary would also be grateful if the gang would refrain from using her glasses and crockery for ink and paint pots. This little practice is quite ruinous, as it is almost impossible to remove the stains.

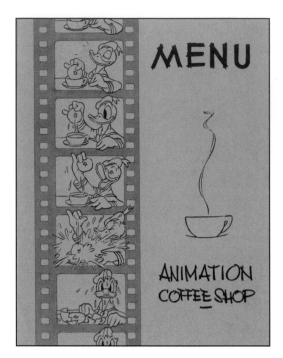

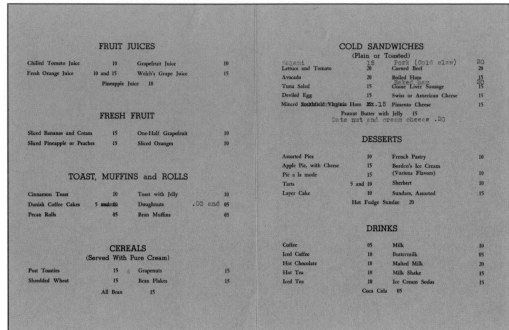

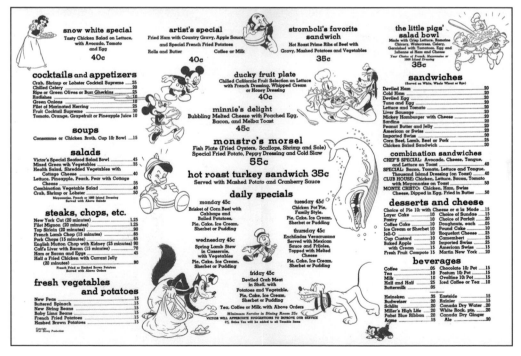

{OPPOSITE, BOTTOM LEFT} *The Studio Café, the temporary restaurant on the Live Action Stage.*

{OPPOSITE, BOTTOM, RIGHT} *The cafeteria line after the 1963 remodel of Studio Restaurant.*

breakfast suggestions

No. 1—25c
Choice of Cereal or Juice
Wheat or Buckwheat Cakes with
Maple Syrup and Butter
Coffee, Tea or Milk

«●»

No. 2—30c
Choice of
Orange, Tomato, Pineapple or Grapefruit Juice
Wheat or Buckwheat Cakes with
Choice of Two Eggs, Bacon, Ham or Sausages
Hashed Brown Potatoes
Coffee, Tea or Milk

«●»

No. 3—35c
Fruit or Fruit Juice
One Egg Any Style with Bacon, Ham
or Sausages and Hashed Brown Potatoes
Toast or Rolls
Coffee, Tea or Milk

«●»

No. 4—40c
Fruit, Fruit Juice or Cereal
2 Eggs Any Style,
with Bacon, Ham or Sausages
Hashed Brown Potatoes
Toast or Rolls
Coffee, Tea or Milk

FRUITS
Baked Apple with Cream 15
Sliced Bananas with Cream 15
Berries in Season 15
Half Grapefruit 10
Sliced Oranges 10
Sliced Pineapple 10
Stewed Prunes 10
Melons in Season 15

FRUIT JUICES
Orange Juice 10   Grapefruit Juice 10   Tomato Juice 10
Pineapple Juice 10   Grape Juice 15

POST'S CEREALS
All Cereals Served with Cream
Hot Cereal 15   Grape-Nuts 15   Grape-Nut Flakes 15
Whole Bran Shreds 15   Post Toasties 15
Post Bran Flakes 15   Huskies 15

EGGS, OMELETTES, ETC.
Two Eggs: Fried, Scrambled, Boiled or Poached 25;
with Ham, Bacon, or Sausage 40
Shirred Eggs (2) 25   Plain Omelette 25   French Toast 25
Fried Ham 25   Rasher of Bacon 20   Link Sausages 25
French Lamb Chops 50   Corned Beef Hash 25; with Poached Egg 30

Toast and Potatoes with Above

HOT CAKES AND WAFFLES
Wheat, Corn, or Buckwheat Cakes with Syrup and Butter 15
Cream Waffle 20
Waffle or Cakes with Ham, Sausage, Bacon or Two Eggs 35

TOAST AND ROLLS
Toast with Jelly 10   Milk Toast 20   Cinnamon Toast 15
Hot Rolls with Jelly 10   Pound Cake 10   Hot Muffins, each 05
Coffee Cake 10   Doughnuts, each 05   Sweet Rolls 10
Strawberry Preserves 10   Orange Marmalade 10

BEVERAGES
Coffee 05   Tea 10   Postum 10   Sanka 10
Milk 10   Chocolate 10   Buttermilk 05

3% Sales Tax will be added to all taxable items

good morning!

WHAT'S GOOD ABOUT IT?

WALT DISNEY'S STUDIO RESTAURANT
BURBANK CALIFORNIA

Mary was released from the studio in August 1941, and with her departure the Animation Coffee Shop closed. Her temporary exit (she was rehired in a different capacity a year later) corresponds with an August 7 memo to Roy Disney from Victor proposing cost-saving measures throughout the Restaurant Department:

> Close Mary Flanigan's, except for cigarettes and candy. No food or drinks whatsoever to be served at this location. Eliminate all room service. There are now 5 people employed in the coffee shop and 5 or 6 traffic boys handling the room service. As a matter of fact, this spot could be closed entirely and cigarette and candy machines installed in the corridors, thus eliminating all expense and making the room available for other purposes.

The space later became a conference room.

THE PENTHOUSE
1940–1979

"The Penthouse Club is not a closed thing. We would be glad to allow any fellow who is decent and respectable to belong to it. However, at the start we had to allow those men who carry the main responsibilities of the Studio the first chance to join. After giving those men their chance, we then threw it open to the whole group."
—Walt Disney

Disney Legend Ruthie Tompson, a painter (with a side job selling peanut brittle made by Walt's Aunt Charlotte to fellow studio workers during Christmas time), who was later promoted to supervisor of the Scene Planning Department and worked on every Disney animated film until she retired in 1975, recalls how Walt wanted The Penthouse completed before other buildings at his new studio. "He wanted to have The Penthouse built first on the Animation Building. He wanted it to be finished because he wanted to stay all night and be here in the morning when they started to work.

"So his wife told a story," Tompson continued. "The Penthouse was finished, and he couldn't wait. He came over to spend the night. And it was fun; he could read his books and manuscripts and all those things. But the only thing was, when he finally got to sleep, it was time to get up. Because all the saws and the buzzers and the whirring things were going and it woke him and he didn't know where he was. It scared him, and he went home and went to bed. That's the last time he spent the night in The Penthouse, so I heard."

The Penthouse was an exclusive fraternity on the Animation Building's private fourth floor. The 1943 Employee's

{ABOVE} *The Penthouse bar and lounge*

MENU

PENT HOUSE
❖ CLUB ❖

FRUIT JUICES

Chilled Tomato Juice	10	Pineapple Juice	10
Welch's Grape Juice	15	Kraut Juice	15
	Tomato & Clam Juice Cocktail	15	

HEINZ SOUP and CRACKERS   15

Tomato	Bean	Vegetable	Mushroom	Green Pea
	Chicken Noodle	Clam Chowder	Vegetable Beef	
	Chicken with Rice		Turtle	

TOAST

Cinnamon Toast	10	Toast and Jelly	10

COLD SANDWICHES

Lettuce & Tomato	20	Peanut Butter & Jelly	15
Tuna	15	Avocado	20
Corned Beef	20	Deviled Egg	15
Goose Liver Sausage	15	Boiled Ham	15
	Ham & Cheese	25	
	American, Swiss, or Pimiento Cheese	15	

SALADS   25

Tuna and Tomato	Lettuce and Tomato	Fruit Salad
	Pineapple and Cottage Cheese	

PRESERVED FRUITS   15

Figs	Prunes	Peaches	Pineapple	Pears

ICE CREAM and COOKIES

Vanilla or Chocolate Ice Cream	10
Chocolate, Pineapple, Caramel, or Strawberry Sundae	15

BEVERAGES

Coffee	05	Tea	10
Iced Coffee	10	Iced Tea	10
Hot Chocolate	10	Milk	10
Malted Milk	15	Buttermilk	05
Milk Shake	15	Coca Cola	05
Canada Dry Ginger Ale	10	7-Up	05

BEERS

Heineken's Holland Beer	35	Acme Beer	15
Miller's High Life	20	Acme Ale	15

{ABOVE} *Walt (far right) with his attorney, Gunther Lessing (far left), eating lunch at The Penthouse in 1940.*

Manual mentioned, "Men only! Sorry, gals!" The member roster was a who's who of studio executives and animators and a perk for higher-ranking and higher-paid male employees. Animator and Disney Legend Ollie Johnston recalled, "The Penthouse probably caused some problems. They had to draw the line somewhere, because there wasn't room for everybody, so you had to be making a hundred dollars a week to join The Penthouse, and that really bugged some people."

Inside the exclusive club's walls were a restaurant, bar, gymnasium, massage tables, steam baths, billiards, card tables, barbershop, and beds that were used mostly by those overserved the night before. Outside on the roof were tables, umbrellas, and mattresses where men could sunbathe to get an all-over tan. This ritual continued until a new wing for St. Joseph Hospital was erected across the street, providing a compromising view for the nurses and nuns. The Mother Superior called the studio requesting the men don their trunks, and for the most part, they did.

Food was an important component of The Penthouse. In 1959, Victor asked Penthouse members to complete a survey and received these responses: "Try Fish and chips. Try *fresh* fish and chips," one member wrote. "Yes, broil everything—and you asked for it from a guy loaded with gallstones," from another.

Baked ham led the way as the preferred dish, followed closely by fried chicken and corn bread, hamburger, steak, pot roast, and Swiss steak. The least popular dishes were stuffed cabbage and baked tuna.

The Penthouse's restaurant closed in 1979 and after that was primarily used as a gathering place for the old guard.

INKING & PAINTING
CAFETERIA AND TEA LOUNGE

The work performed in the building with these locales was mostly unheralded, yet critical for animation. The "Inkers" were responsible for taking the finished animation drawings and tracing them in ink on transparent cels. The "Painters" used opaque paint, often mixing it themselves, on the reverse side. The department was nearly exclusively made up of women. They were not allowed to go to the male-dominated Animation Building unless they had business there. To be fair, it was a patriarchal era, and although the Inkers and Painters were never credited in the films, paternal Walt cared about their comfort.

Betty Kimball, a painter and the wife of animator Ward Kimball, one of the Nine Old Men and a Disney Legend, described the Inking & Painting Building as "a wonderful place." She noted, "Walt had real new ideas about what working space should be. And he had all the furniture designed by someone special...we had ideal working conditions. And everything was in color. It was beautiful."

In the April 16, 1940, memo, "Discussion of New Burbank Studio" by Frank Crowhurst, the concept of the structure's cafeteria and tea lounge is explained:

> There is a restaurant over the Paint Lab that will be adequate to serve all the girls. It is a very luxurious, first-class layout. It is going to have its own kitchen, own dishwashing department, own soda fountain, besides a very large open dining room. The girls, however, will secure their food like they would in a cafeteria. Go to the counter and get whatever they want, buffet style. The idea Walt has is most of the girls will like a bowl of soup or a bottle of

milk, and then take it to their table and have sandwiches they have brought with them. For those who haven't, there will be one main dish, roast beef or country sausage—something that could come over from the main restaurant. The girls have a very, very fine lounge there, too, so they can lie down. It is almost a club room, in a way, inasmuch as it is entirely reserved for them.

The "very, very fine lounge" was called the Tea Lounge, and not the Coffee Lounge, because the high caffeine content of coffee would make the hands of the Inkers (whose skills were considered the most deft) shake. It was beautifully decorated with soft-toned carpets and walls, and furnished with brightly patterned divans and chairs. The cafeteria was painted in coral, gray, and bright chromium. There was a private sundeck, just like The Penthouse, but it was used for resting and rejuvenation, not sunbathing.

Painter Dodie Roberts recalls, "Walt loved the Paint Lab. He loved to show off the colors. And one time, you know, we had what we called 'Tea Time,' because there was a tearoom upstairs. So I was standing at the door yelling 'tea time' and I turned

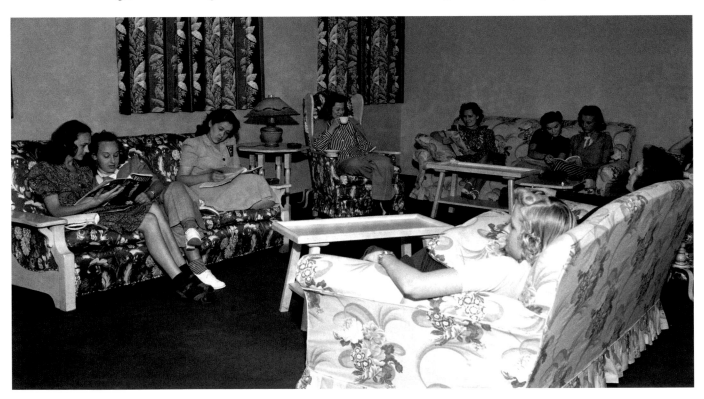

{ABOVE} *Inkers and Painters relaxing in the Tea Lounge*

{OPPOSITE} *Coral Room waitresses with Cecile Van Antwerp, last on the right.*

around and there was Walt with a smile on his face. And I said, 'Oh we don't have to go, we can stay and show you.' He says, 'I know my way around. Go ahead.' So we did. He loved that Paint Lab. It was beautiful to see all those colors on the shelves."

Sometimes, however, Walt would come upstairs to join the women for tea. Tompson recalls, "Walt thought a lot of us and he was always visiting us, to see how we were doing and give us a chuck under the chin, make us feel all happy, you know. He'd come up and have tea with us sometimes. And visit and sit around and chat with the different people. Or whoever had an empty seat at their table, there he was, talking to 'em. So he was real friendly with all of us."

There is one treat that will be forever associated with the lounge—Martino's tea cakes. The square buttermilk cupcakes with a sugar glaze were provided by Martino's Bakery.

Even though the Tea Lounge is gone, the tea cakes remain incredibly popular with past and present employees—and fans—of the Walt Disney Studios.

CORAL ROOM
1956–1986

Walt ate almost daily at the commissary for fifteen years; however, by 1956, a year after Disneyland opened and the *Mickey Mouse Club* debuted on television, it became apparent Walt would need a private dining room. Mostly as a place to entertain executives and VIPs, although some would say it also provided a respite from stage mothers. The menu was more upscale than the menus at the Studio Restaurant and the Coffee Shop. In addition to soups and sandwiches, there were elegant daily specials such as Poached Colorado Brook Trout with Hollandaise and Scallopini Picante. The waitresses wore long skirts, crisp white shirts, and tight coral belts along their waists.

Shorty after the Coral Room opened, Cecile Van Antwerp was hired as a waitress. She loved her job, which was evident by the testimonials from customers who raved about her winning smile and excellent service. In 1963 Cecile and her husband were in a horrific car crash near Las Vegas. After the accident, she was rendered a quadriplegic with a grim prognosis. Walt sent a plane to medevac her to what was then Van Nuys Presbyterian Hospital near her home close to Burbank, and later that December sent a limousine full of Christmas presents for her children.

Cecile was transferred to the Motion Picture & Television Country Home where she remained two years before her final rehabilitation at Rancho Los Amigos in Downey, California. After three years of hospitalization, all expenses taken care of by Walt, Cecile returned home. Upon this momentous occasion Walt made her an honorary Silver Retiree at Disney, a distinction that normally required twenty-five years of service. Any time she wanted to visit the studio or Disneyland, a

Walt Disney's Studio Restaurant

Coral Room

BURBANK · CALIFORNIA

CORAL ROOM

Tuesday, March 13 th.

Potage Saint Germain - Chicken Broth
Jellied Consomme - Cold Vichysoisse
Juice or Salad

Special Salad of the Day - Ala Carte
Avocado Stuffed with Chicken Salad   1.95

E N T R E E S
Scallopini Picante   1.95
Roast Sirloin of Beef, Au Jus   1.95
Sweet & Sour Spare Ribs, Hawaiian   1.95
Maryland Scallops, Saute Meuniere   1.95
Poached Colorado Brook Trout,Hollandaise 1.95
Half Broiled Spring Chicken   1.95
       with Spiced Peach
Omelette Fines Herbs   1.75
Hot Corned Beef Sandwich, Garni   1.50
       on Kaiser Roll

Carrots Vichy   Whipped Potatoes
Creamed Spinach   O'Brien Potatoes

Choice of Dessert and Drink

chauffeured car was sent and Cecile was given star treatment.

Walt exuberantly passed out cigars in the Coral Room when his namesake grandson was born in December 1961. Son-in-law Ron Miller explains, "We named our firstborn Chris because we didn't think any child of ours should lead a life being named Walter Elias Disney Miller.

"Then Walt let us know that there is nothing wrong with the name Walt Disney. And we more or less had an agreement with Walt that the next boy was going to be named Walt," Miller recounts. "After Chris we had Joanna. Then we had Tammy. Then we had Jenny. And we were about to leave the country, and then the big event—Walter was born."

WALT'S OFFICE

While Walt could be found frequently in the commissary and Coral Room, just as often he would eat at his desk. According to Lillian, "Lunch was usually just a sandwich, milk, coffee . . . he always wanted coffee for lunch."

Walt's offices, in the 3H wing of the Animation Building, consisted of three main rooms. A formal office (where part of his miniature collection was displayed) also housed the piano, a working office (where he held most of his meetings) featured a galley kitchen (which, when it wasn't in use, was concealed by wooden doors matching the paneling in the office that could be slid together).

A carafe of coffee was waiting on Walt's desk every morning, though that first carafe was rarely fully consumed. In a Walt Disney Archives interview, his secretary Tommie Wilck recalled, "He used up the whole carafe. He poured it out and then it got cold and he'd call for one of us to come and pour out his cold coffee and pour in some hot coffee and it would be too hot so he couldn't sip it and it'd sit there for a while—and we went through that all morning. . . ."

Adding to the coffee lore, when Walt had coffee, everyone had coffee. He drank it throughout the day, and as anyone who ever had a meal or a meeting with Walt can attest, they were served coffee whether or not they wanted it or had the time for it. Cream and sugar were not offered. And if it wasn't touched, it was taken to go. Always.

There were two rituals—one at noon and one a half hour later. At 12:00 Tommie would serve V8 juice to everyone in the office, and like the coffee, it wasn't an option. "[Columnist] Hedda Hopper was the only one who wanted to know if she was expected to drink the stuff straight," Tommie said.

At 12:30 Tommie would ring a bell, an award to Walt from the Coast Guard, to signal lunchtime. "One day when he was in a very good mood, and someone he knew was in the office, and I was trying to get him to go to lunch, I came in and gave the bell a 'clunk' and somehow or the other he really liked that idea.

{ABOVE} *Walt and guests being served lunch from inside the office kitchen.*

{OPPOSITE} *During World War I, Walt remembered once making himself custard with powdered milk and powdered eggs. He left it to cool, only to return to find several British airmen finishing the last of it. Walt was surprised in his office when Wing Commander. L.V. Harcourt of the Royal Air Force and Dr. J.K.S. St. Joseph (far left and left, respectively) represented the British Air Ministry with the repayment of the custard debt twenty-six years later. Animator and director Wilfred Jackson looks on (right).*

"From that time on, at twelve-thirty, we came in and gave the bell a good clang—then he would say to his guests, 'It's time to go to lunch.' I only did it for fun and games," remembered Tommie. "He picked up on it, it really did become a part of each day—at twelve-thirty, if we hadn't rung that bell, he was just as apt to give the intercom a couple of clicks and let you know it was time he left for lunch at twelve-thirty."

It was in this office that Walt allowed a rare interview with Mickey Mouse in 1947. Frank Nugent of *New York Magazine* made the request, and even though Walt said it was "a little irregular" he played along. Pressed with the queries about Mickey's annual salary, family background, and political leanings, Walt kept to generalities:

> I've always done the Mouse's talking. [He never calls Mickey by his first name; he's always the Mouse just as Donald is the Duck.] He's a shy little feller, so I provided the voice. I use a falsetto, like this. [And he demonstrated.] His voice changed after I had my tonsils out. It became a little deeper. But no one noticed it. I kind of like it better. Sometimes I am sorry I started the voice. It takes a lot of time and I feel silly doing the Mouse in front of the sound crew. But I am sentimental about him, I guess, and it wouldn't be the same if anyone else did the speaking.

A short time after this interview, Walt turned the voicing of the Mouse to Jimmy Macdonald, one of the studio's resident sound effects wizards.

Tommie further noted the significance of other times throughout Walt's workday. "Five o'clock was drink time in the office. If you were in the office at five o'clock, we always served drinks. Walt always had a Scotch mist and I always served whatever anybody else wanted," recalled Tommie to writer Richard G. Hubler.

Toward the end of Walt's life, he'd occasionally invite songwriters Robert and Richard Sherman to his office on Friday for the evening ritual. He'd ask Richard to "play it." There was no question what "it" was—his favorite song, "Feed the Birds," from *Mary Poppins*. The lyrics give insight into Walt's benevolence—his belief that small kindnesses go a long way. Disney Legend and lyricist Robert Sherman once explained the sentiment: "Doing just a little extra and going just a little bit out of your way to make someone feel special. Sometimes it makes all the difference in the world to a person."

> *Come feed the little birds, show them you care*
> *And you'll be glad if you do*
> *Their young ones are hungry, their nests are so bare*
> *All it takes is tuppence from you….*

When the song was finished, Walt would say under his breath, as an aside to himself, "Yup. That's what it's all about."

Robert overheard that whisper and concluded, "I do think this song summed him up. He was just a simple man—a simple, wonderful man who understood that the greatest gift life bestows upon a person is the chance to share with others."

{OPPOSITE} *Walt and Roy celebrating Father Elias's birthday in the Studio Restaurant.*

Chapter 3
WALT'S DISNEYLAND: MAIN STREET, U.S.A.

Main Street, U.S.A. is America at the turn of the century—the crossroads of an era.
The gas lamp and the electric lamp—the horse-drawn car and the auto car.
Main Street is everyone's hometown—the heart line of America.
—WALT DISNEY, JULY 17, 1955

ICE CREAM 15¢

Main Street, U.S.A. is a gateway and a land unto itself, along with Adventureland, Frontierland, Fantasyland, and Tomorrowland. It is fashioned in part from Walt's fond boyhood memories of Marceline, Missouri. It was there he played along the tracks of the Santa Fe Railroad, drawing farm animals on any scrap of paper he could find. Walt was encouraged when a country doctor offered to buy one of his sketches for twenty-five cents; he later acknowledged that it was that early sale that persuaded him to pursue his artistic abilities.

The Disney family moved away from Marceline four years after they arrived, but the time Walt spent there had a profound effect on him. "More things of importance happened to me in Marceline than have happened since . . . or are likely to in the future," he said.

Main Street, U.S.A. is more a manifestation of Walt's emotional attachment to Marceline than an authentic re-creation. It was designed to represent any small town in America at the turn of the last century. The leisurely pace was characteristic of the era, with horse-drawn carriages, a market where townsfolk gathered to gossip and shop, an old-fashioned ice cream parlor, bakery, and eateries typical of the day. Walt intended it to be nostalgic, patriotic, immersive, and realistic.

Imagineer and Disney Legend Marty Sklar was a student editor at UCLA when he was hired at Disneyland the summer of 1955. He was assigned to write the 1890s-themed *Disneyland News* tabloid. Walt was personally involved in the project, but Marty was hard-pressed to understand how he had the time to "worry about this little thing, a ten-cent newspaper to be sold on Main Street." It was just days before Disneyland would open and there were hundreds of other details to attend to, but soon Marty realized why. "It was a story and a detail. That's what Disneyland is about, stories and details."

For Walt, Main Street, U.S.A. was a real place. Every small town in America had a paper, and Walt's town would have one, too.

CARNATION ICE CREAM PARLOR
July 17, 1955–January 15, 1997
Carnation Company is proud to have been selected by Mr. Walt Disney as the exclusive supplier of dairy products in fabulous Disneyland.
—Carnation Ice Cream Parlor menu

Walt envisioned the Carnation Ice Cream Parlor as a gathering spot for Guests of all generations. "It's a living memory for some, a new adventure for most," according to the *Independent-Press-Telegram*. The menu quipped that, "Just about the only thing that isn't as it was fifty years ago is the ice cream." Authentic Victorian details included hand-cut mirrors framed in Honduran mahogany, with the hardwood authentic to the 1890s. The tables and chairs were wire-backed with leather-tufted seats. Maintaining the Victorian feel while updating for twentieth-century businesses presented a conundrum for Main Street's art director, Wade Rubuttom. Business establishments in the period had dim interior lighting, which would be inadequate for modern merchandising. Wade's solution was to use old fixtures with bright contemporary lights fitted on the inside. The soda fountain counter was marble, also true to the era; yet hidden underneath there was twentieth-century technology—refrigeration.

Carnation turned to Bob Gurr, who created the "Car of the Future" for Autopia, asking for a "Truck of the Past." It didn't take long for Bob to determine that finding a vintage vehicle in suitable condition was nearly impossible, so he began

working on plans for an authentic "antique" of the 1910 era. Starting with a Model A chassis, he added Model T wheels and designed the body by following guidance provided in his old automobile book, A*ntique American Cars* by Floyd Clymer. He also sought out old automobile magazines in the studio's library. Carnation built the truck in their own service shop in Glendale. The Carnation Wagon was an instant hit from day one, though Walt had one objection: the plaque behind the driver's seat read CARNATION. Walt knew hundreds of pictures a day were taken of kids sitting behind the wheel, so he had it replaced with one that said DISNEYLAND.

A few years later Bob pointed out to Walt that Main Street had a firehouse, but no fire engine. Walt's response was, "You're right, Bobby," and a few hours later the purchase order was approved. (Walt had to request purchase orders just like everyone else.) Bob designed the 1910-style replica and it became one of Walt's favorite vehicles. In August 1966, it would be a featured prop in one of the last photographs taken of Walt at Disneyland. He was behind the wheel, grinning ear to ear, with the Mouse riding shotgun.

{OPPOSITE, BOTTOM} *Swift Market House concept art by Dorothea Redmond, 1964*

SWIFT MARKET HOUSE
JULY 18, 1955–1965
"In sunny California we won't be able to have get-togethers over a hot stove like the old days, but we ought to be able to trade plenty of ideas anyway."
—Myrt Westering, Manager

Swift Market House portrayed the retail meat and grocery business of Gustavus F. Swift. It was maintained as a historical exhibit, evoking the feel of the stores of yesteryear, which served as meeting places much as mercantiles did. The large potbellied stove in the center of the room had chairs surrounding it, an invitation for the weary to rest and share a tale or two. There was a checkerboard, bins for staples, and two vintage coffee grinders—the smaller of which was used to grind fresh coffee beans daily. Although most of the shelves were lined with decorative canned and packaged foods, the dill pickles were real, plucked from the brine-filled vat and wrapped in butcher's paper for the Guests. Penny candy, particularly horehound, was also a popular item. Old-fashioned, wall-mounted telephones allowed eavesdropping on a party line conversation and Guests might hear: "And just to think, thirteen cents a pound for meat!"

C&H SUGAR MARKET HOUSE
1965–1970
After Swift's contract ended in 1966, the Market House became a mercantile operated by C&H Sugar. Suggested names were Sugar Corner, Sweet Shop, The Candy Jar, Candy Arcade, C&H Candy Counter, and C&H Sugar House Confectionary.

Ultimately they kept it simple, incorporating the company's name and the name of the original 1955 building.

Main Street, U.S.A. maintains a small yet fascinating example of the ingenuity applied as the locale was being created. When the electricians installed the sockets for the red and white ceiling lights in 1955, they used an odd number. When it was time to screw in the bulbs, they discovered they were one socket short. To keep the red/white pattern going, the Imagineers used a low-tech solution: paint one bulb half red and half white. When you visit the park, find the special bulb, which was left untouched in the 2015 remodel.

MAIN STREET STATION RAILROAD REFRESHMENT STAND
JULY, 1955–CIRCA 1965

In the earliest discussions about Disneyland's creation, long before there was even a location picked in Anaheim, California, there was Walt's one constant: "It will be surrounded by a train." On Opening Day, the Disneyland and Santa Fe Railroad had two locomotives running, both named for pioneers of the Santa Fe Railway, the corporate sponsors of the attraction. Engine No. 1 was the *C. K. Holliday*, named for Cyrus Kurtz Holliday (and inspired by drawings of Walt's one-eighth-scale *Lilly Belle* locomotive, the centerpiece of his Carolwood Pacific home railroad). The *E. P. Ripley*, engine No. 2, was named for Edward Payson Ripley. The theming for both trains reflected the image of the station/land they served: the *Ripley*, with ornate yellow cars, reflected a Main Street, U.S.A. exuberance, while the *Holliday*, pulling stock cars and gondolas, exuded a more rugged Frontierland sense.

United Paramount Theatres (known as UPT, a division of the American Broadcasting Company, which made a substantial loan to Disneyland and aired the *Disneyland* television program on their network) operated several stands and carts in Disneyland, including one inside the Main Street Station's

COCA-COLA REFRESHMENT CORNER
JULY 17, 1955–PRESENT

The Coca-Cola Refreshment Corner was an exhibit and a restaurant affectionately known as "Coke Corner." Coke was king, of course, but Guests could also buy sandwiches and snacks to enjoy on the patio overlooking the Plaza.

While many exclusives were granted for food products at Disneyland, that wasn't the case for carbonated beverages. Most notably, Pepsi-Cola was the sponsor for The Golden Horseshoe. Coca-Cola, however, retained the right to have at least one outlet in the other four lands—including next door to Pepsi's saloon in Frontierland—as well as in Adventureland, Fantasyland, and Tomorrowland.

What was Walt's preference? Coke or Pepsi? The answer is in the list of provisions stocked in his Disneyland apartment. (See page 84.)

The entrance to the Coca-Cola Refreshment Corner on

depot. The original 1955 contract limited the concessions to hot dogs, sandwiches, popcorn, candy, ice cream, ice water novelties, coffee, milk, and soft drinks, "[but] no other items without the prior approval of Disneyland."

SUNNY VIEW FARMS
JULY 17, 1955–DECEMBER 1958

Sunny View Farms was both an exhibit and a store. With the exception of Welch's grape products, which were being sold in Fantasyland, Sunny View had the exclusive right to sell jams, jellies, preserves, and marmalades at Disneyland. They also sold fruit—fresh, candied, and preserved.

PUFFIN BAKERY
JULY 18, 1955–JUNE 3, 1960

Every small town in America had a bakery with tantalizing treats on display, and Main Street, U.S.A. was no exception. Puffin was a division of the Ready to Bake Foods Company and one of the originators of "icebox" cookies—rolled and refrigerated dough sliced into rounds that were then baked. In addition to selling their packaged goods, Puffin's lease required a "live bakery" on the premises. Contractually they were allowed to make biscuits, muffins, and Parker House rolls, and expressly prohibited from making hot dog or hamburger rolls. Similarly, they could make layer cakes in several flavors but not angel food cake, pound cake, or cheesecake. (Most likely these restrictions were because of noncompete clauses with other purveyors.)

Overseeing this operation was master baker Bill Lane, a forty-year baking veteran well known throughout Southern California. He was a towering man who specialized in decorating cakes. After graduating from the Wilton School of Cake Decorating in Chicago, he had the honor of making a piano-shaped cake for President Harry Truman. Lane eventually brought this prowess to Disneyland, where he decorated cakes to order at Puffin—everything from Mickey Mouse to Donald Duck, and even ones baked in the shape of Sleeping Beauty Castle.

CANDY PALACE
JULY 22, 1955–PRESENT

The Candy Palace, also known as Candyland in the early days, had cotton candy pink walls and was operated by the A. R. Brooks Corporation, a Los Angeles-based company that specialized in butter-toffee nuts. The first shop didn't have a kitchen on the premises. It sold fudge that was prepared off premises and then cut and packed on the shop counter. When a large kitchen was installed, it wasn't hidden in the back; it was placed in front. Senior candymaker Lee Hight explained, "It's the show of making candy they [the Guests] really enjoy." And if they couldn't see the show, they could smell it. Scents were purposely vented out onto Main Street, U.S.A. to attract Guests. After *Mary Poppins* was released in 1964, "A Spoonful of Sugar" became the shop's signature song.

{ABOVE} *Candy Palace concept art by Dorothea Redmond, 1965*

MAXWELL HOUSE COFFEE HOUSE
DECEMBER 1, 1955–OCTOBER 8, 1957

"A Maxwell House on Disneyland's Main Street, U.S.A.
The authentic charm of the old south will be recaptured here. . . .
It's expected that Maxwell House will be a favorite place
for Disneyland's visitors to tarry for a moment's relaxation
and a cup of delicious Maxwell House Coffee."
—Disneyland News, July 1955

The official opening of the Maxwell House Coffee House had all the excitement of a Hollywood premiere. Celebrities Eve Arden and Dean Miller attended, as did Walt even though he had a terrible case of laryngitis. Despite buckets of rain, the cancellation of the planned parade, and the postponement of Walt's award as "Greatest Guy in the World," the dedication ceremonies in Town Square went off without a hitch.

Following the ceremonies, two hundred of the Guests boarded the train at Main Street Station for the brief ride to the Frontierland Station, while others followed the Disneyland Band to the Plaza. Everyone came together again for dinner and entertainment at the Chicken Plantation Restaurant. Maxwell House VIPs were then treated to an after-party at the Red Wagon Inn.

The lavishly appointed café resembled a turn-of-the-century New Orleans hotel. Its ornate lobby was decorated with crystal chandeliers and plush velvet furniture. The ceiling resembled the midnight blue sky, fading in and out with twinkling lights. Besides their "Good to the Last Drop!" coffee, pastries, cakes, ice cream sundaes, and JELL-O were served. Maxwell House was the official coffee at Disneyland, served exclusively throughout the park, until Hills Brothers took over the lease in June of 1958.

HILLS BROS COFFEE
JUNE 13, 1958–WINTER SEASON 1976

We certainly hope your visit to Disneyland will be
an exciting moment in your life. We think it will be,
so we invite you to take this Hills Bros. Coffee House
menu with you as a souvenir of a happy time—maybe
one of the happiest times you've had anywhere.

The Hills brothers, Austin H. and Ruben W. (known as R. W.), were innovators just like Walt. In 1900, R. W. originated the process for vacuum packing; it's still the most widely used method of packaging coffee today. And after twenty years of research, the brothers brought instant coffee to the market in 1956.

In addition to their signature coffee and Danish pastry, the menu featured the "Surprisingly Good" sandwich made of nut bread, toasted fruit, and Philadelphia cream cheese. The "properly seasoned" chopped egg sandwich was also popular.

SUNKIST CITRUS HOUSE
JULY 31, 1960–JANUARY 3, 1989

Sunkist was welcomed to Main Street on July 31, 1960. Citrus House inhabited the space previously occupied by Puffin Bakery and its neighbor to the left, Sunny View Farms Jellies and Jams. Walt was present at the ribbon-cutting ceremony along with Sunkist's advertising manager, Russell Z. Eller, who proudly declared that "Sunkist and Disneyland are synonymous with California." More than five thousand Guests attended. The curved juice bar featured freshly squeezed orange juice and lemonade, along with what was billed as the "World's Freshest Lemon Pie." A novelty was introduced to the park: frozen juice bars. They were sold at the Sunkist Citrus House and throughout the park, instantly becoming as popular as ice cream bars. Sunkist orange and grapefruit gift cartons

The Maxwell House
DISNEYLAND
MENU

Cup of Delicious Maxwell House Coffee....10
Refreshing Maxwell House Iced Coffee......15
Crystal Clear Maxwell House Iced Tea......15
Bakers, Rich and Smooth Ice Cold Chocolate
   with Whipped Cream and Wafer......20
Steaming Pot of Maxwell House Tea.......15

SPECIALTIES

Homemade Danish Pastry (served warm)....20
Assorted French Pastry (your choice)......35
Chocolate Eclairs, Custard Filled...........25
Cocoanut Delight 20
Superb Cheese Cake 30
Fancy Jell-O Topped with Whipped Cream..20
Hot Fudge Ice Cream Cake..............40
Fresh Strawberry Ice Cream Cake.........45
Old Fashioned Strawberry Shortcake......35
Cream Puffs, Custard Filled...............25

"Good to the Last Drop!"

"The Greatest Guy in the World"

The man who takes his family OUT to dine
Maxwell House
at DISNEYLAND
MENU

Delicious Maxwell House Coffee	.10
Refreshing Maxwell House Iced Coffee	.15
Steaming Pot of Maxwell House Tea	.15
Refreshing Maxwell House Iced Tea	.15
Baker's Rich Hot Cocoa	.20
Baker's Ice Cold Chocolate Flavored Drink	.20

SPECIALTIES

Apple Sauce Cake	.15
Homemade Danish Pastry (served warm)	.20
Superb Cheese Cake	.30
Old Fashioned Strawberry Shortcake	.35
Assorted French Pastry (your choice)	.35
Hot Fudge Ice Cream Cake	.40

JELL-O DESSERT

Fancy Jell-O Gelatin topped with whipped cream	.15

Printed in U.S.A. 8329

Menu

HILLS BROS. COFFEE HOUSE

—THE COFFEE BREAK—
Fluffy light Mocha Cake
Baked exclusively for Hills Bros.
Coffee house — complemented by
delicious Hills Bros. coffee
—50c—

FANCY PASTRIES FROM THE TRAY

WARM DANISH ROLLS	30c
MOCHA LAYER CAKE	45c
OLD FASHIONED APPLE TURNOVER	45c
DISNEYLAND CHEESE CAKE	45c

BEVERAGES

COFFEE MOCHA	35c	POT of TEA	15c
HILLS BROS. COFFEE	15c	HOT COCOA	25c
CARNATION MILK	15c	ICED TEA	20c

5% sales tax will be added to price of all food & beverage items served.

Welcome to Hills Bros Coffee House and Garden

A GOOD CUP OF COFFEE

What is a good cup of coffee?

We believe it is a great deal more than something hot to drink.

It is courage in the morning. Refreshment at noon. Congeniality with friends along the afternoon's way. And restoration when the day has ended.

It cheers the gloomy, wakes the sleepy and soothes the tired. It is drink for the body; food for the spirit too.

And when you brew Hills Bros. Coffee, you can be sure that all these goodnesses are there in overflowing measure. For 82 years, three generations of the Hills family have devoted their efforts to providing you with coffee that is delicious, deeply satisfying and always uniform in quality.

We are insistent on the same standard of quality in our instant product. We have purposefully made it to be the instant that is most like good, rich ground coffee in the cup.

When you lift a cup of Hills Bros. Coffee to your lips, you enjoy the alluring aroma, the dark golden-brown color, and the rich, deep satisfaction you associate with good coffee and all it means to you.

And that is true whether you buy your Hills Bros. Coffee in the instant or ground form. Because both are made by the same people, with the same care, and following the same aim:

To give you a good cup of coffee every time.

INSTANT OR GROUND
HILLS BROS

SWIFT'S RED WAGON INN

JULY 17, 1955–OCTOBER 11, 1964

*"There are two kinds of people—the ones who have
already been up and at 'em and are now willing to relax
and enjoy a sturdy meal, and those who are in a hurry
to be on their way and do everything at Disneyland.
The menu at the Red Wagon Inn caters to both."*
—Myrt Westering, General Manager, Red Wagon Inn

The Red Wagon Inn was a "luxury restaurant at popular prices" designed to be reminiscent of the glamorous 1890s. Walt wanted families to have a fancy dining experience where they could feel special and comfortable. As with all buildings at Disneyland, it was authentic to the era thanks to Walt's purchase of an opulent 1870s mansion located in the posh St. James Park neighborhood of Los Angeles. The home was scheduled to be demolished to "make room for progress" when Walt dispatched his head decorator and Disney Legend Emile Kuri to salvage everything useful from the estate.

The original materials were used throughout Disneyland, though the Red Wagon Inn showcased the most dramatic pieces, including a stained glass ceiling and leaded cut-glass entrance doors. The diners were seated in one of two lavish atriums on the east and west sides of the restaurant.

The Red Wagon Inn got its name from the red horse-drawn delivery wagon icon of the lessee, Swift's Premium Foods. In addition to complete meals, the menu offered favorites of Walt, such as hash, tuna sandwiches, and hamburgers. There was something for everybody—breakfast, lunch, or dinner.

were shipped anywhere in the United States—the only way to get California fruit if you didn't live in the state at the time.

In the wee hours of the mornings, before the park opened, Walt used to walk down from his apartment and "break in" to the Citrus House. (He didn't own it, Sunkist did.) Walt would get behind the counter and operate the modern machines, making orange juice for himself and the workers on Main Street. Despite the self-service he always insisted on paying.

It occurred to the shop's manager, Bo Foster, to give Walt an electric juicer for his Disneyland apartment. He arranged for Walt's secretary to alert him anytime Walt would be in the park, ensuring that there would always be plenty of fresh Sunkist oranges in his kitchen. While that was convenient, it didn't stop Walt from the fun of sneaking into the Sunkist Citrus House, playing with the automatic extractors, and passing out juice to his predawn crew.

{ABOVE} *Walt in the Sunkist Citrus House*

{OPPOSITE} *Long lines for the Red Wagon Inn, July 1955*

Red Wagon Inn

Disneyland
ANAHEIM, CALIFORNIA

CAST CAFETERIA/THE INN BETWEEN
1956–Present

Disneyland's first employee or "Cast" restaurant, and the only one serving the graveyard shift, was located in the rear of the Red Wagon Inn, "in between" Main Street, U.S.A. and Tomorrowland. The cafeteria (originally a tent with a "roach coach") got its punny name in 1969, acknowledging both its location and in-betweeners—the artists who fill in the images between the animator's principal drawings.

THE HIDEOUT
1955–1967

Even though Swift's name was on the door, Walt had a small private room in the back of the Red Wagon Inn behind the east atrium. The not-so-secret door, with its colorful stained glass accents, can be seen on the Tomorrowland side of the restaurant. It was lightly used until Goodyear sponsored the PeopleMover in 1967 and started using it as their VIP lounge.

PLAZA INN
July 18, 1965–Present

"Buffet dining in the grand Victorian manner has been brought by Walt Disney to Disneyland with the opening of his Plaza Inn Restaurant on Main Street Plaza, one of the highlights of Disneyland's year long Tencennial Birthday Celebration. Lavish applications of luxurious red brocades, gleaming crystal, dramatic stained glass, and generous use of mirrors create the magnificent Victorian atmosphere in the antique-studded foyer and the two large dining rooms."
—Walt Disney Imagineering press release

Walt had taken possession of many of the lessees' restaurants by 1965. The Red Wagon Inn, its grandeur long lost, was the most ambitious remodel. The design was overseen by one of Walt's Renaissance men, Imagineer and Disney Legend John Hench. The intention was to return the restaurant to its Victorian splendor, only this time in Disney style. The custom appointments included a gilded Louis XV wall clock and sixteenth-century Parisian cabinet that held a collection of Lillian's personal dinnerware. Hench added the Hidden Mickey touch in the scalloped eaves.

Several sit-down dining concepts were discussed, including making the Plaza Inn two separate and distinct restaurants—a prix-fixe buffet on one side and a steakhouse with an à la carte menu on the other. Offering fried chicken in the park again was considered a high priority (the popular Chicken Plantation was closed in 1962). Ultimately it became a "no-menu, no-check" smorgasbord where Guests could make their own selections and pay quickly, avoiding "time-consuming chores" of ordering and waiting for a check. The 1965 press release describes the fare as "a pageant of food arranged on rare Norwegian marble in buffet style.

TENCENNIAL 1965!
THE MAGNIFICENT PLAZA INN
OPENS

DINING ON THE PLAZA
RECEPTION AND SERVING KITCHENS..

{ABOVE} *Plaza Inn concept art by John Hench, 1964*

{OPPOSITE} *Walt plucks fruit from the antique gold, three-tiered epergne as John Hench looks on.*

There were two five-foot-diameter, three-tiered servers garnished with a variety of salads. Each was crowned by a glittering antique gold epergne that had been converted into a fountain.

"The rotisserie offers barbecued or roasted meat and fowl," the release proclaimed, "and nearby are beautifully appointed tables of subordinate courses, along with spreads of extravagantly decorated desserts."

Innovation wasn't reserved solely for the dining rooms. A hidden bussing apparatus with a two-hundred-foot-long conveyor ferried dirty dishes to an underground kitchen. Although forward-thinking, it proved to be inefficient. It was easy for Cast Members to get the dishes down, but when it came to hoisting the bins of clean dishes back up to restaurant level, the system failed. Also hidden and an important addition was the large in-house bakery that could serve all of Disneyland's food facilities.

The Plaza Inn shared its Opening Day with Great Moments with Mr. Lincoln. While it was initially an E-ticket for adults, Walt invited all Guests seventeen and younger to attend the attraction for free, "So that young people may become better acquainted with one of the greatest figures in American History." The poster displaying the offer to the youngsters and an advertisement for the Plaza Inn still hangs in the Opera House lobby.

One of Walt's personal touches remains in the restaurant. He wanted to hang birdcages near the windows in the solariums. Health codes prohibited his feathered friends from singing for their supper. The hooks, however, were never removed, a tribute to Walt at his favorite restaurant in the park.

PAVILLION
JULY 17,1955–JULY 17, 1960

STOUFFER'S PLAZA PAVILION
SUMMER 1962–MARCH 1963

The Pavillion, with two "l's" (and later known as the Plaza Pavilion with one "l"), featured two separate facades: it was Victorian on the Plaza side in keeping with Main Street, U.S.A.'s theme, and Polynesian on the Adventureland side, blending in with the tropical atmosphere. It was open seasonally: summer, Easter, Thanksgiving, and Christmas.

Two outside companies operated it briefly. First, beginning on Opening Day, was Grand Central Concessionaires. Their original lease called for a "walkaway-type cafeteria, wherein patrons will be able to obtain a complete meal at each station." Guests were encouraged to enter from the Plaza side, select their food, then exit to Adventureland to sit and eat. It was touted as "a completely new conception of high-quality, low cost food service."

In 1959 Grand Central Concessionaires added the "exotic" Hawaiian Broiler, a large open rotisserie with chicken and ribs turning on the spit. It was the first thing Guests saw when they entered the Pavillion; at night the glowing embers could be seen from outside the restaurant. One of the principals, Milt Wollis, enthused, "We know that this touch of authenticity will greatly enhance the Pavillion and make it another 'must' on the already long lists of 'musts' at Disneyland." This may have been a last-ditch effort for Grand Central Concessionaires, whose food was considered to be lackluster; when their five-year lease expired in 1960, Disneyland took over the floundering eatery.

Chief Art Director and Disney Legend Richard "Dick" Irvine led the team refurbishing the Pavillion. In an internal report, it was concluded that there was no basic concept or theme:

As, for example, we sell in one end of the room hot dogs, hamburgers, snacks, etc.; in the middle of the room we have [a] cafeteria-type operation; and in the other end we have a so-called Polynesian[-] or Hawaiian-type service. None of these particular operations have an entity of their own or are so well conceived and so well operated that they leave any impression on our Guests.

It was clear that the quality, value, and variety of offerings were going to be greatly improved. "We envision in this room a high-quality, but modestly-priced, Buffeteria-type of service for those who wish to serve themselves but do not want hamburgers or hot dogs," the report stated. "We firmly believe that there are enough places in Disneyland for people to secure hot dogs and hamburgers without this service to be included in the Plaza side of the Pavillion operation." The suggested menu items included soups, melons in season, spaghetti with meat sauce, chicken potpies, beef stew with vegetables, French dip sandwiches, buttered green peas, baked beans, mashed potatoes, and an assortment of desserts.

Despite these in-house plans, Stouffer's was brought on board in 1961; they were as well-known for their chain of restaurants as their frozen food. And with this change, one of the "l's" was dropped from Pavillion, and the establishment ultimately became the Plaza Pavilion. Stouffer's proposal called for the Main Street side to be a cafeteria with two kitchens—one for American fare and the other for European. A whimsical and iconic mural was put in the center of the restaurant,

{ABOVE} *Plaza Pavilion concept art by John Hench and Bruce Bushman, 1961*

73

with homey images of bygone appliances in black juxtaposed with enticing tasty treats that were shown in color.

Among the Plaza Pavilion concepts developed, although never implemented even in its reincarnation, was a proposal to have two lines in the cafeteria: one would be for parents and stocked with "adult food," and the other would be for children, with age-appropriate offerings. While Mom and Dad made their selections, a hostess would assist the kids and bring them back to the table to join their families.

Although it was never realized, in part because of con-

cerns about Stouffer's staffing costs, it demonstrates Disneyland's commitment to innovation. The short-lived arrangement with Stouffer's Foods ended in April 1963, prompting Walt's friend Joyce Hall—of Hallmark Cards Company fame—to write this letter:

> Hearing that the Stouffer arrangement at Disneyland didn't work out has given me concern. It is a little baffling to me that Vern [Stouffer], who is so capable at running a string of good eating houses, did such a

{ABOVE} *The Pavillion, two "l"s, in 1955*

bad job at Disneyland. You may recall my recommendation to him and to you at the start of this . . . that he serve his frozen foods there and publicize them in the process. Then, if he only broke even, it still would have been a terrifically good institutional promotion for him. With this kind of operation, the quality and variety of the food served would be controlled and, as you probably know, his frozen foods are excellent. I suppose it is too late now to do anything about it, but I still think this plan would have worked advantageously for everyone concerned.

Walt thoughtfully replied:

You shouldn't be upset. There's nothing wrong with their food and their restaurants. But their method of operation just wasn't compatible to Park procedures. Their local people had no authority. Everything had to come from Cleveland and our people had no jurisdiction either. So it didn't work out for our purposes, but the divorce was a friendly one. I was disappointed, too, but we've taken it over and I think we will be able to give the public the kind of food and service they want.

Walt and Hall's long friendship began in 1932 when they first signed a licensing deal to produce greeting cards—the same year that Silly Symphony's *Three Little Pigs* was released. Although Gibson Greeting Cards was selected as the original lessee in 1955, Hallmark eventually opened a shop on Main Street, U.S.A. in 1960. In his book *When You Care Enough*, Hall explains how three little girls he met on an intercontinental flight expressed his feelings about Walt better than he ever could:

I asked if they had a good time in London, and one said, "Yes, but we would have rather gone to California." Surprised, I wondered why. The oldest girl answered, "To see Disneyland and Burbank." And what did they want to see in Burbank? She said, "Walt Disney." She knew his studio was there. I asked if they thought Walt Disney was a real man or someone more like Santa Claus. The oldest girl thought this over carefully and answered, "Both." And I agreed with her.

CARNATION PLAZA GARDENS
August 18, 1956–September 13, 1998

Situated on the Plaza under a giant red-and-white circus-like tent, this was the second shop for Carnation. (A root beer garden was once considered for this location.) Vanilla ice cream was popular as was rainbow, fresh peach, and pineapple. A custom flavor was created by Carnation just for Disneyland—Fantasia—which was a blend of burgundy cherry, banana, and pistachio. The restaurant also served burgers, sandwiches, and hot dogs.

Imagineer and Disney Legend Tony Baxter's first job was at Disneyland, a short bike ride from his childhood home. He was seventeen, and with Disneyland's policy of only hiring employees eighteen years and older, found work with lessee Carnation. He was ambitious—to launch his career with Disney—not in refreshment concessions. Tony idolized Walt and was waiting for the day he'd get to meet him and pitch a few ideas. That opportunity presented itself in 1965 when Cast Members were alerted

{THIS SPREAD} *Carnation Plaza Gardens*
concept art by Herb Ryman, 1963

Carnation in Disneyland

SANDWICHES

Cheeseburger .... 55c   Hamburger 45c
With Lettuce, Tomato, Pickle and Relish.
American Cheese (Grilled or Plain) 30c
Ham (Grilled or Plain) 50c
Ham and Cheese (Grilled or Plain) 60c
Tuna Salad 40c
Hot Dog (Premium Frank with
Tasty Pickle Relish) 25c

*All Sandwiches Delightfully Garnished with
Dairy Fresh Carnation Cottage Cheese.*

SALADS

Cottage Cheese with Choice of
Pineapple, Pears or Peaches 65c
Fruit Bowl with Sherbet,
Banana and Whipped Cream 65c
Crisp Green Salad 65c

SPECIALITIES

Soup of the Day 25c
Chili and Beans 40c
Cheeseburger Size 70c

PIES and CAKES

Pie .... 20c   Pie a la Mode 35c
Cake .... 20c   Cake a la Mode 35c

BEVERAGES

Milk (half-pint) 10c
Buttermilk (half-pint) 10c
Chocolate Drink (half-pint) 10c
Coffee 10c
Tea (Iced or Hot) 10c
Coca Cola 10c
Pepsi Cola 10c
Sarsaparilla 10c
Phosphate (Cherry or Lemon) 10c
Root Beer 10c
Welch's Grape Juice 15c

The word "Carnation" is the registered
trademark of Carnation Company.

FEATURES FROM FRONTIERLAND

Golden West Float 30c
An invigorating Orange Freeze.

Log Cabin Sundae 40c
A tasty Caramel Sundae topped with a miniature log cabin of pretzel sticks.

Sante Fe Express 60c
Miniature choo-choo, 3 scoops of ice cream,
strawberries, pineapple, chocolate, banana
wheels, marshmallow, whipped cream and
cherry.

Old Timer 40c
An old-fashioned treat made with Pepper-
mint Stick Ice Cream, strawberries, pineapple, whipped cream and cherry.

TREATS FROM Fantasyland

Castle Special 79c
Castle with 5 scoops of ice cream, marshmallow topping, 2 whole bananas.

Snow White Sundae 35c
Marshmallow sundae topped with grated
coconut.

Mad Hatter Sundae 25c
Small chocolate sundae garnished with salted peanuts.

Carnation in Disneyland Special 79c
One of the world's largest sundaes. 5 scoops
of ice cream, sliced pineapple, 5 different
sundae toppings, sliced banana, chopped almonds, whipped cream and cherry.

Peter Pan Sundae 45c
3 scoops of chocolate ice cream, marshmallow topping, chopped almonds, whipped
cream and cherry.

SURPRISES FROM TOMORROWLAND

T. W. A. Rocket Ship Special 75c
Space Ship ready to blast off, 4 scoops of
ice cream an ice cream cone, cherry and
marshmallow toppings, and banana.

2000 A.D. Special 45c
We predict that health foods will never replace this tasty treat . . . a delicious hot
fudge sundae.

Inter-Planet Special 45c
2 scoops vanilla ice cream, topped with fruit
salad, whipped cream and cherry.

Martian Sundae 45c
2 scoops of vanilla ice cream, hot caramel
topping, sprinkling of malted milk powder,
sliced peaches, whipped cream and cherry.

IMPORTS FROM Adventureland

Hawaiian Sundae 50c
Vanilla and strawberry ice cream with pineapple, strawberries, coconut, sliced banana
and sliced pineapple.

Amazon Special 55c
Hot fudge over 2 large scoops of vanilla ice
cream, banana, chopped almonds, whipped
cream and cherry.

Tropical Sundae 55c
Tasty treat made with 2 scoops of ice cream,
quartered banana, pineapple topping,
whipped cream and cherry.

Tahitian Sundae 40c
2 scoops of vanilla ice cream, with chocolate
topping and salted peanuts.

SUGGESTIONS FROM MAIN STREET

Old Mill Strawberry Sundae 35c
Two scoops of Vanilla Ice Cream, covered
with fresh frozen strawberries, whipped
cream and cherry.

Victorian Banana Split 55c
Vanilla, chocolate, strawberry ice cream,
topped with strawberries, pineapple, banana,
chopped almonds, whipped cream and cherry.

Gay Nineties Sundaes 35c
Chocolate, Caramel, Cherry, Pineapple,
Marshmallow.
Junior Sundaes 25c

Old Fashioned Ice Cream Sodas 30c
Vanilla, Pineapple, Lemon, Chocolate, Root
Beer, Coffee, Strawberry, Cherry.

Town Square Malted Milks or Shakes 35c
Vanilla Pineapple, Coffee, Chocolate, Root
Beer, Strawberry and Cherry.

Gibson Girl Parfait 45c
3 scoops of ice cream with fresh frozen
strawberries, almonds, whipped cream and
cherry.

Almond-Marshmallow Sundae 40c
2 scoops of chocolate ice cream, with marshmallow, chopped almonds, whipped cream
and cherry.

Cimarron Sundae 40c
Vanilla and strawberry ice cream, strawberry
and pineapple topping, chopped almonds,
whipped cream and cherry.

Lovers' Delight 40c
Strawberry and vanilla ice cream, marshmallow and strawberry topping, chopped
almonds, whipped cream and cherry.

Hot Caramel Sundae 45c
2 large scoops of vanilla ice cream, with hot
caramel, chopped almonds, whipped cream,
and cherry.

Black and White Sundae 45c
Chocolate and vanilla ice cream with marshmallow and chocolate, chopped almonds,
whipped cream and cherry.

Tandem Dish of Ice Cream 25c

(Please Do Not Ask For Substitutions)

We Feature Swift's Premium Meats, Maxwell House Coffee, Van Camp Tuna

CARNATION IN DISNEYLAND

Greetings from Carnation in Disneyland! We hope you will be able to visit us personally soon. Here you can relax in a reproduction of a typical ice cream parlor of the Gay Nineties period. The wire chairs and marble-topped tables, the mirrored backbar behind the fountain—all are authentic in design. Just about the only thing that isn't as it was over fifty years ago is the ice cream. And you'll agree that today's ice cream is better than ever! That's because in every spoonful of Carnation ice cream is the experience of more than half a century in producing the finest quality foods.

Toward the end of the 1890's, Carnation Company was founded in Kent, Washington, near Seattle, by Elbridge Amos Stuart, a former Los Angeles wholesale grocer. The first product was Carnation Evaporated Milk, today the world's largest selling brand.

Early in the 1900's, Mr. Stuart established Carnation Milk Farms, where the famous Carnation line of Holstein-Friesian dairy cattle was developed. The ability of these animals to produce extraordinarily large quantities of milk has been introduced into dairy herds across the nation and in many foreign countries. Farmers almost everywhere are benefiting as the result of this Carnation dairy research.

From a single plant operation in 1899, Carnation now has more than 150 spotless processing plants and receiving stations in the United States and Canada, employing over 10,000 men and women. The Carnation product line includes a complete selection of fresh dairy products, both home and store delivered, ice cream and frozen novelties, malted milk, instant milk and mix for chocolate flavored drink, a variety of Albers breakfast cereals, mixes, livestock, and poultry feeds, Friskies pet foods, Simple Simon brand frozen pies, cakes and cookie rolls.

Research into new products and new methods is carried out at Carnation Research Laboratory, Van Nuys, California, one of the best manned and equipped in the industry. You can rest assured that when you use products of Carnation Company, you are using the finest.

Maps and Information About Disneyland, Available at 4,000 Richfield Stations Throughout the West.

that Walt was in the park and all service windows should be manned, as he might want a snack or ice cream. As it turned out, Walt walked into Carnation and asked Tony how things were going. Totally overwhelmed, and with his sharp mind going blank, all Tony could manage was, "Fine, just fine, Mr. Disney."

"My main goal was to switch over to attractions. Which I did," recalls Tony. "Looking back I think working in foods is more fun, because you had camaraderie about it. Whereas working on attractions was a very responsible job, and if you weren't watching what you were doing, people could get injured. So you didn't goof off and laugh and all the stuff you can do in an ice cream parlor."

In January 1967, Tony brought his conceptual sketches for a *Mary Poppins* attraction to work. He showed them to a few people, and with the help of a supervisor, the drawings made their way to Disneyland's president, Dick Nunis; he arranged for Tony to meet Imagineering recruiters. Several years later the rest became park history, with Tony's major creative contributions to Disneyland including Star Tours, Big Thunder Mountain Railroad, Splash Mountain, and the Indiana Jones Adventure.

HOW TONY BAXTER SINGLE-HANDEDLY RAISED THE PRICE OF ICE CREAM AT DISNEYLAND

Management needed the price-to-product relationship to establish the correct ice cream pricing. They looked at all the scoopers and determined that Tony had the most consistently sized scoop. "My cones looked nice, my cones looked sculptural. A lot of guys did big 'ol globs. Something that five seconds later a Guest would have all over their arms," recalls Tony. He was tasked with scooping an entire carton of vanilla ice cream and counting the number of balls. The carton wholesaled for $6.95 and Tony got sixty balls out of it, making it evident that at ten cents a scoop they were losing money—and

that didn't count the labor and the cones. As a result, Disneyland increased the cost of ice cream to fifteen cents for a single scoop and twenty-five cents for a double scoop.

PANCAKE RACES
1957–1964

The Pancake Race tradition dates back to the fifteenth century. According to English legend, on Shrove Tuesday, the day before Ash Wednesday, a woman in the town of Olney was making pancakes using the last of her cooking fats—forbidden during Lent. She was so engrossed with her whisking and flipping that when the church bells tolled, she ran out of the house with her apron on and skillet in hand. While it may have been an unconventional entrance to the sacred shriving ceremony, the idea caught on: Shrove Tuesday became known as Pancake Day, with apron-clad women racing to church with skillets ever since.

The Quaker Oats Company brought the obscure food-related footrace to Main Street, U.S.A. after it began recruiting cities across America to host "Aunt Jemima Pancake Days." Tommy Walker, director of Entertainment (who had also notably pulled double duty back in his college days at the University of Southern California as the Trojan's Drum Major and placekicker on the school's football team), and Eddie Meck, publicity manager, recognized the obvious tie-in with Aunt Jemima's Pancake House in Frontierland. Eager for inexpensive entertainment in the era before daily parades and fanfare, the two modeled their contest after a similar race held annually in Liberal, Kansas.

Beginning in 1957, housewives outfitted in long skirts, sensible shoes, and aprons vied for one hundred dollars in cash and prizes. Each contestant carried a nine-inch skillet containing one pancake. Four times during the sprint, a contestant

had to flip, or fling, her pancake over a stretched ribbon eight feet in the air (the height of a regulation volleyball net). If she didn't catch her pancake in her skillet on the other side, she was disqualified. The 415-yard course, which required navigating the streetcar tracks, started in Town Square, traveled down Main Street, and then circled the Plaza before the finish.

Aunt Jemima, who was portrayed by Palmere Jackson, presided over the event, along with celebrities Clarence Nash, the voice of Donald Duck, *Mickey Mouse Club* host Jimmie Dodd; and judges Mel Patton (world record holder in the 100- and 200-yard dashes) and his coach, track and field hall of famer Dean B. Cromwell.

WALT'S APARTMENT

"It was their refuge, it was their little place. The decor, it was all little things that they picked up when they were traveling around the country various times, and it was decorated by Emile Kuri, who had decorated many of the films, including 20,000 Leagues Under the Sea, and it was lovingly done. It was really a very cozy, family place."
—Diane Disney Miller

Located above the Firehouse, the one room and one bath apartment was a private home for Walt, Lillian, and their family. Keeping with the Main Street theme and their love of the era, the decor was Victorian, with Lillian's favorite cranberry red as the dominant color. The sitting area had a television, an old-fashioned Victrola, chairs, and two large foldout beds that did double duty as couches. The tiny galley kitchen had a refrigerator, grilled cheese press, toaster, ice bucket, butler's tray, and a Tom and Jerry serving set. Walt and Lillian enjoyed entertaining there. A 1959 memo listed the supplies to be stocked in the apartment:

1 Dubonnet
1 Brandy (Courvoisier or Martel 4 Star)
2 Wolfschmidt Vodka
2 Beefeaters Gin
3 Yellowstone Bourbon
6 Black & White Scotch
1 Harvey's Bristol Cream
12 Canada Dry Club Soda—Small
12 Coca Cola
12 7-UP
6 Canada Dry Quinine Tonic Water—Small
6 Cans Miller's High Life
12 Small Cans V-8 Juice
3 cans Smorgasbord Peanuts—from Candy Palace
3 cans Smorgasbord Assorted Nuts—from Candy Palace

Diane reminisced how her dad liked to have friends up to the apartment: "During *Davy Crockett*, I remember there was some event there that day and Fess Parker and Buddy Ebsen were both out there for it, and Dad was looking out that window and saw them and he said, 'Hey, come on up!' He told them how to get around, back behind, and get up to the apartment . . . [where] there was a door into the closet area that had a fire pole, like the firemen would have, and he showed it to them and said, 'Why don't you guys slide down that?' And they did! People would say, 'Did your father ever do that?' I'm sure he didn't."

The fire pole remains from Walt's second floor apartment down to the firehouse. The opening was sealed long ago to block Guests from looking up to catch a glimpse of their hero.

In preparation for Opening Day, workers reportedly recalled seeing Walt's apartment window lit long into the night. And although he passed away on December 15, 1966, the lamp remains lit in tribute to the man that created the Happiest Place on Earth.

Chapter 4
WALT'S DISNEYLAND: ADVENTURELAND

Here is adventure. Here is romance. Here is mystery. Tropical—silently flowing into the unknown. The unbelievable splendor of exotic flowers . . . the eerie sound of the jungle . . . with eyes that are always watching. This is Adventureland.
—WALT DISNEY, JULY 17, 1955

Walt's love of nature and his True-Life Adventures film series were the inspiration for Adventureland. During Disneyland's construction, he instructed the landscape architects to, "Grow a jungle. It has to look like the tropics and like deepest Africa, and like Australia and Asia, and the Amazon." Orange trees, which had been uprooted a year before when construction began on the site, were replanted upside down, with the bromeliads on top, to simulate the primitive and exotic look Walt wanted.

There was only one Adventureland attraction in 1955—Jungle Cruise. Initially, Walt was determined to have real animals. However, he soon realized how impractical it would be, despite his desire to share nature up close with his Guests; this practicality spurred the development of mechanical and Audio-Animatronics.

One piece of history remains at the attraction since then: a palm tree from Disney Legend and former Disneyland Vice President Ron Dominguez's front yard. Ron grew up on the property that became Disneyland. His family home, situated roughly where Pirates of the Caribbean stands today, was sold to the park in 1954. The house was moved backstage and became an administration office; the palm tree that his grandparents planted in 1895 was relocated to the Jungle Cruise queue.

ADVENTURELAND TROPICAL
SALOON AND CANTINA
CIRCA 1955–1962

Lawson Engineering operated the cantina and saloon within the Adventureland Bazaar. Along with merchandise from tropical areas around the world, they sold coffee, soft drinks, and natural fruit juices, including the "exotic" papaya, coconut, and pineapple. Their lease allowed them to sell snacks such as potato chips, nuts, cakes, and cookies; however, hot dogs and hamburgers were expressly prohibited.

THE TAHITIAN TERRACE
JUNE 1962–APRIL 17, 1993
Welcome to the wondrous realm of Polynesia . . .
the Tahitian Terrace! Here Walt Disney has opened the
portals to an enchanting island world across the blue Pacific . . .
a world of romance, beauty, and exciting entertainment!
—Tahitian Terrace menu

The Tahitian Terrace, (originally operated by Stouffer's before Walt decided their involvement was problematic) was nestled behind Walt Disney's Enchanted Tiki Room on the banks of the Jungle Cruise's Jungle River. Taking over the Adventureland space once used by the Pavillion, the Terrace was a sit-down restaurant serving a variety of Cantonese and Tahitian dishes along with the incongruous franks and beans, chicken potpie, and the ever-present hamburgers and hot dogs. In the summer there was a dinner show featuring a water curtain, grass-skirted dancers, and barefooted fire walkers.

The centerpiece of the stage was a thirty-five-foot-high tree, known as the Disneydendron Semperflorens Grandis, ("large ever-blooming Disney tree" in Latin), that "grew" in one year thanks to a secret formula developed by Walt and his Imagineers. Whatever the formula was, it wasn't right the first time. Marty Sklar fondly recalls a survey of the site with Walt and the head of construction, Joe Fowler. Walt didn't think the tree was high enough; he wanted the dancers to be seen in plain view. Joe didn't seem to know what to do when Walt chimed in, "You know, Joe, this isn't a real tree. You can take out the center and add three feet."

When completed, the Disneydendron had over fourteen

{OPPOSITE} *Tahitian Terrace dancers perform under the Disneydendron.*

Dinner Menu

4 P. M. TO MIDNIGHT

DISNEYLAND'S

Tahitian Terrace

hundred handcrafted leaves and flowers and provided shade for a significant part of the restaurant. It was the second highest of the four man-made trees at Disneyland, along with the tallest, the Swiss Family Treehouse (now Tarzan's Treehouse), the Blue Bayou restaurant tree, and the tree house on Tom Sawyer Island. Although the Disneydendron was an attraction in itself, and had Walt's personal imprint, it was removed after the Tahitian Terrace closed.

SUNKIST, I PRESUME
June 1962–January 20, 1989

When the Adventureland Cantina closed in 1962, Sunkist took over the space across from the Jungle Cruise and Swiss Family Treehouse. Cast Members referred to it as "I-P." In addition to their signature orange juice, they served Jungle Juice, a thick fruit concoction that came in a small cup.

WALT DISNEY'S ENCHANTED TIKI ROOM
June 23, 1963–Present

"Pay attention. It's showtime!"—José, parrot host

Walt Disney's Enchanted Tiki Room, which opened on June 23, 1963, was initially conceived as a Chinese restaurant just off Main Street, U.S.A. When that location was abandoned, Walt envisioned a dinner theater in Adventureland. According to Disney Legend and studio machinist Roger Broggie, Walt said to his Imagineers, "I want to have a Chinese restaurant at the park. Out in the lobby will be an old Chinese fellow like Confucius—not an actor, but a figure. Now the customers will ask him questions, and he'll reply with words of wisdom."

And thus, the first ever Audio-Animatronics human head was for a Chinese man, and not Mr. Lincoln, as most people believe. Yet there are two theories: The first suggests it was just

a coincidence. Bob Gurr recalls that engineer Jack Gladish had been working on a full-sized human head on and off beginning in 1956; it was more of a passion project for him than an assignment. When Walt saw it working—the eyeballs in the metal substructure following him around the shop—he was excited and intrigued. The limitations of latex and technology at the time, however, made it a challenge, and with necessity being the mother of invention, the resulting experimentation produced a head that appeared Asian to Walt. And so in this version it was Gladish's tinkering that was the inspiration for a Chinese restaurant at Disneyland.

Theory two is that the head of the Confucius character was built deliberately. However, when the restaurant concept was nixed in 1961, so was the fabrication of his body. Regardless, all this experimentation led to the first fully realized Audio-Animatronics human, the lead in Great Moments with Mr. Lincoln, which debuted at the New York World's Fair in 1964.

Two of Walt's travel adventures helped shape the attraction. A trip to the South Seas, which introduced Walt to the Polynesian culture, and a trip to New Orleans, where Walt purchased an antique mechanical bird in a cage. He was enchanted by the bird's ability to move and sing and brought it back to his Imagineers to reproduce and improve.

Imagineers next studied the recently declassified Polaris missile technology to control the numerous complicated functions of the show, including utilizing multichanneled magnetic recording tape to synchronize the birds singing and movements. The massive computers that controlled each and every bird were housed in air-conditioned rooms below the showroom floor. (Today the entire show can be controlled on a single smartphone.)

It was known in development as the "Enchanted Tiki and Bird Room," or simply "The Bird Room." This excerpt from the attractions "Basic Theme Outline" explains Walt's vision in 1962:

{OPPOSITE} *Enchanted Tiki Room restaurant concept art by John Hench, 1962*

For the first time in his entertainment career, Walt Disney is creating a restaurant. And just as his full-length motion pictures, true-life adventures, and magic kingdom of Disneyland pioneered in their fields, Walt's creation may alter the course of many full course meals . . . this summer, in association with one of America's foremost restaurateurs, Stouffer's Foods, Disneyland will unveil Walt's "new concept" in elegant dining . . . "Stouffer's Enchanted Tiki and Bird Room." The show has been designed to astonish, surprise, excite[,] and entertain, with the emphasis on surprise entertainment as Tikis, flowers[,] and birds that appear to be merely solid or stuffed figures suddenly "come to life" and perform. All the techniques of animation, Audio-Animatronics and other special effects used in Disneyland will be utilized to make the dinner show truly unique and "one of a kind"—perhaps another forerunner in the entertainment field for Walt Disney.

A mock-up of the Enchanted Tiki and Bird Room was constructed on Stage 3 at the studio.. When executives from other companies visited, Walt liked to show off his talking bird. Sometimes he would ask his friend and star of The Golden Horseshoe Revue, Wally Boag, to interact with his Guests as the voice. (Wally was later cast as the show's host, José.) Then it would come time for Walt to tell his favorite joke: "What's a four-letter word for what's at the bottom of his bird cage?" Everyone would look at each other, wondering if Walt Disney was going to say *that*. And just when the tension was getting thick, Walt the on-color jokester would say, "Grit. Grit!"

The outline went on to explain that reservations would be offered in hourly intervals for 140 Guests at a time. "A set menu . . . one price . . . one service." Guests would be advised to arrive fifteen minutes before their appointed time to enjoy the "Garden of the Gods" reception area, where sarong-clad hostesses would serve drinks and appetizers. Maui the God of Time would ring his gong, signaling it was dinnertime. Guests would be ushered into the dining room, where the main course would be preset on the tables. Once everyone was seated, the hostesses would remove the covers and diners would have thirty minutes to complete their meal. The suggested menu included French-Fried Shrimp, Sweet 'n' Sour Ribs, "Oriental" Fried Rice, and a California version of almond chicken.

Dessert, Fresh Coconut Angel Cream Cake, would be delivered right before the performance began. At its conclusion, Guests were to exit promptly, making room for the next group waiting in the lobby.

It soon became obvious, however, that diners would tend to linger under the animated birds once the show ended, thus making it impossible to achieve the table turnaround needed to make the restaurant profitable. Or as John Hench famously quipped, "It can't be a restaurant. The birds will poop on the diners."

Two components of the eatery were built before the concept was abandoned, yet remain today: the service area in the center of the four-quadrant room under the Bird Fountain (with cupboards below that still open and close) and the restrooms in the Enchanted Tiki Garden (a California requirement for sit-down restaurants).

It's called Walt Disney's Enchanted Tiki Room because initially Walt owned it, financing it privately through his company WED, an acronym for Walter Elias Disney (and now called WDI or Walt Disney Imagineering). The attraction was sold to Disneyland on the day it opened.

To recoup the investment, and prior to the A through E ticket system, an admission charge of seventy-five cents was set. To entice Guests, an Audio-Animatronics "Barker Bird" (named Juan and also voiced by Wally) was installed outside the attraction to pitch the show inside. He was so intriguing, however, he stopped traffic and the entrance to Adventureland was perpetually blocked. To ease the congestion, the Barker Bird was removed, but only briefly. He was soon reinstated, not because of improved traffic patterns, but at the Cast Members' behest—they preferred that the bird did all the talking.

{OPPOSITE, TOP} *Chinese host concept art by Herb Ryman, 1966*

{ABOVE} *Chinese restaurant (to have been located off Main Street, U.S.A.) concept art by Herb Ryman, 1958*

Chapter 5

WALT'S DISNEYLAND: FRONTIERLAND

Here we experience the story of our country's past . . . the colorful drama of Frontier America in the exciting days of the covered wagon and the stage coach . . . the advent of the railroad . . . and the romantic riverboat. Frontierland is a tribute to the faith, courage and ingenuity of the pioneers who blazed the trails across America.

—Walt Disney, July 17, 1955

Frontierland was the largest of the lands on Opening Day, occupying nearly one-third of the park. Its time frame, set between 1790 and 1880, was created to celebrate America's pioneering spirit and the brave citizens who forged their way west in covered wagons and stagecoaches. Walt was as nostalgic about this land as he was about Main Street, U.S.A. It was also the location of the most restaurants, many of them sit-down eateries, something that was scarce in Fantasyland and Tomorrowland.

THE GOLDEN HORSEHOE
July 17, 1955–Present
DINING – LIBATIONS – STAGE SHOWS
ALL IN ONE PLACE
LADIES ARE WELCOME
OUR DECORATIVE APPOINTMENTS WERE BROUGHT AT
GREAT EXPENSE
BY TREACHEROUS VOYAGES AROUND THE HORN
BEST FOOD. BEST SHOWS
IN THE TERRITORY

Designed by Disney Legend Harper Goff, The Golden Horseshoe was an elaborate replica of typical saloons one would find throughout American frontier towns during this era, and a faithful reproduction of the set *Calamity Jane* set, also designed by Goff. The bar had the "tallest glass of pop" and it was made very clear that only nonalcoholic drinks were to be served at Disneyland. Art Director Herb Ryman, a Disney Legend famous for drawing the first concept map of Disneyland in one weekend, recounted his discussion with Walt just before the opening of the The Golden Horseshoe: "Walt asked about the whiskey bottles on the back bar. I said, 'They are bottles of the turn of the century. I think it has a very good feeling of authenticity.'

"Walt," he recounted, "said, 'We've got to change the labels on those bottles.' When I protested, he said, 'Herb, there are going to be a lot of people coming here. I would like it if they didn't see anything that anyone could disapprove of.' So we changed the bottles."

The Golden Horseshoe's menu featured "Tongue Teasing Food and Drinks." In addition to Pepsi-Cola, courtesy of the attraction's sponsor, three types of sandwiches were available: beef and cheese, ham and cheese, and Chicken of the Sea tuna salad. Fritos, already popular in Frontierland, were also on the menu along with potato chips. It was here that "Calypso" sandwiches were offered exclusively to Cast Members. Calypso was the name of an album made famous by Harry Belafonte in 1956. The sandwich with the same name was a nod to the album's title track (a song about dockworkers—the Rivers of America dock is across the street from The Golden Horseshoe), and the previous day's leftovers, or "Day-O"—day old.

Walt had a private box on the lower right side of the stage (stage left), but being a man of the people, he could just as easily be found entertaining his guests on the main floor. Walt never tired of watching his friend Wally Boag in The Golden Horseshoe Revue. It's estimated that Wally gave almost forty thousand performances over twenty-seven years. He rested between shows in a private dressing room, akin to a small apartment, above the Silver Banjo and Aunt Jemima's Pancake House.

"TEMPUS FUGIT"

Walt used his favorite Frontierland attractions to celebrate his thirtieth wedding anniversary to Lillian. The Tempus Fugit (Time Flies in Latin) party took place on July 13, 1955, four days before Disneyland opened. Prior to dinner in

{OPPOSITE, TOP LEFT} *Walt and Lillian celebrate their thirtieth anniversary with Diane and Sharon on The Golden Horseshoe stage.*

{OPPOSITE, TOP RIGHT} *The Tempus Fugit invitation*

{OPPOSITE, BOTTOM} *The Golden Horseshoe concept art by Sam McKim, 1954*

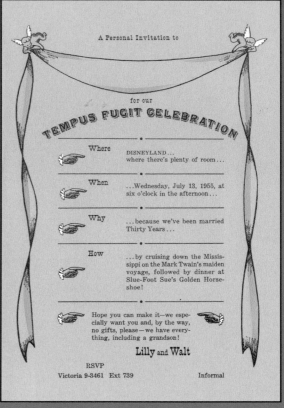

A Personal Invitation to

for our

TEMPUS FUGIT CELEBRATION

Where — DISNEYLAND...
where there's plenty of room...

When — ...Wednesday, July 13, 1955, at
six o'clock in the afternoon...

Why — ...because we've been married
Thirty Years...

How — ...by cruising down the Mississippi on the Mark Twain's maiden
voyage, followed by dinner at
Slue-Foot Sue's Golden Horseshoe!

Hope you can make it—we especially want you and, by the way,
no gifts, please—we have everything, including a grandson!

Lilly and Walt

RSVP
Victoria 9-3461   Ext 739   Informal

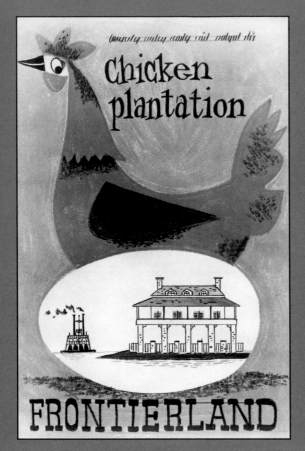

chicken plantation

FRONTIERLAND

Designed by WED Enterprises, Inc.
Copyrighted by Disneyland, Inc.

· SWIFT'S CHICKEN PLANTATION ·

The Golden Horseshoe, party guests sipped adult mint juleps on the Mark Twain's maiden voyage. Walt couldn't wait to show it off to his guests; the riverboat was very special to him. After returning from his service in France as an ambulance driver at the end of World War I, he had planned to sail the Mississippi with his friend and codriver Russell Maas.

But when Russell got married, he backed out on the journey, and the trip was canceled. Walt was not going to miss the opportunity to sail on a romantic riverboat a second time. When funding fell short for the Mark Twain, Walt used his private funds to complete it. The 105-foot-long paddle wheeler was the first one built in America in fifty years. An extensive search was conducted for gimbal lights, smoke bells, and running lights authentic to the period. In the end, it was accurate in every detail, down to the name, which before Walt's hero Samuel Clemens claimed it, goes back to the turn of the century when the leadsmen sang their safety call, "Mark Twain"—meaning the water was twelve feet deep and thus safe for the vessel to proceed.

SWIFT'S CHICKEN PLANTATION
JULY 17, 1955–JANUARY 8, 1962
"The side facing the river has the wide verandas, grille-work, and graceful construction of early century New Orleans. But the opposite side of the building faces a scene from the old southwest—a stagecoach and a railroad station from America's colorful "Iron Horse" era. This side of the restaurant has an adobe motif."
—Independent-Press-Telegram, 1955

The Chicken Plantation, later known more casually as the Chicken Shack, resembled an antebellum river plantation home with French provincial decor. It sat in Magnolia

Park on the bend of the Rivers of America. A footbridge adjacent to the restaurant covered the confluence of the Rivers of America and the river of the Jungle Cruise (now two separate waterways). Fried chicken was its specialty, mostly in response to the adage, "Go to Disneyland for the rides. Go to Knott's [a nearby amusement park famous for Mrs. Knott's fried chicken] for the food." This was Swift's highest capacity draw in the park, with seating for 360 Guests. It was also an event venue of sorts, catering for up to one thousand Guests with portable tables. Walt suggested that barbecues could be brought in for these occasions as long as they were removed when not in use.

The only other Disneyland location that could accommodate large groups was Holidayland, a parklike setting that opened outside the gates in 1957. It was available for rent and offered full catering services provided by Swift. And although Walt forbade any alcoholic beverages in Disneyland proper, wine and beer *were* allowed at Holidayland.

In 1961, with plans under way for New Orleans Square, it became evident that the Chicken Plantation would have to be demolished to make room for the new land—tricky business because the Plantation was Swift's most profitable venue in the park. There were discussions about relocating it next to the Pirate Wax Museum (the original concept for Pirates of the Caribbean). Disneyland executives suggested to Swift that it would be to their benefit to close the Plantation from January to May in 1962, noting the cost savings when winter business was slow; plus, with the Pavilion being closed, they surmised Guests would flock to Swift's Red Wagon Inn. But it was not to be. Chicken Plantation shuttered permanently on January 8, 1962.

{OPPOSITE, TOP LEFT} *Chicken Plantation ad in the* Disneyland News

{OPPOSITE, TOP RIGHT} *The Chicken Plantation viewed from the Rivers of America side*

{OPPOSITE, BOTTOM} *Swift's Chicken Plantation interior concept art by WED Enterprises, circa 1954*

AUNT JEMIMA'S PANCAKE HOUSE
AUGUST 9, 1955–JANUARY 1962

AUNT JEMIMA'S KITCHEN
JULY 17, 1962–1970
"You're sure going to have lots of fun seeing the wonders of
Disneyland. And when you get hungry from all that walking
around, you can sit down and enjoy some Aunt Jemima
pancakes. I'll be serving them to you hot off the griddle—
tender and golden brown, with the flavor folks all over
America say can't be matched. So I'll be seeing you
in my own 'Flavor-Land' at Disneyland."
—Aunt Jemima (portrayed by actress Aylene Lewis)

Aunt Jemima was a nationally known, albeit fictional, personality in mid-century America. Her restaurant was a faithful reproduction of a Southern plantation mansion. The interior was wood-paneled, featuring a massive fireplace with a brass kettle hanging inside it. "Aunt Jemima" cheerfully greeted Guests at the door. The breakfast menu was written with typical Disneyland wit and exclusively themed for Frontierland characters and attractions:

DAVY CROCKETT'S DELIGHT
Real ammunition for real b'or hunters! Hearty enough to fortify any frontiersman for a Frontierland foray. You'll set out a-grinnin' to follow the fun. Four brown-as-a-berry Aunt Jemima pancakes.

SLUE FOOT SUE'S FAVORITE
Crisp as crinoline, light as a plume—a favorite of the Queen of the Frontier! Aunt Jemima's wonderful waffle, delicately browned and cooked to a queen's taste.

MARK TWAIN SPECIAL
Come aboard an old-time Mississippi paddle wheeler and sit right down at the captain's Table for [a] mouth-watering meal of four Aunt Jemima Buckwheat cakes with the true flavor of the Old South.

Quaker Oats operated the restaurant from 1955 to 1967; it was renamed Aunt Jemima's Kitchen in 1962. Disneyland took over day-to-day operations of the restaurant in 1967, with Quaker Oats remaining as a sponsor. The restaurant flipped its final pancake in 1970.

{ABOVE AND OPPOSITE, BOTTOM RIGHT} *Black-and-white concept art for Aunt Jemima's Pancake House's exterior and interior by Sam McKim, circa 1954*

{OPPOSITE, BOTTOM LEFT} *Color exterior concept art for Aunt Jemima's Pancake House by Herb Ryman, 1957*

Throughout the years the friendly face of Aunt Jemima has become familiar to generations of Americans ★ ★ ★

One of America's most outstanding artists, N. C. Wyeth, painted this series of now-famous paintings on Aunt Jemima's early days.

Aunt Jemima's fame began in the days "before the war" when she was cook for Colonel Higbee whose Louisiana plantation was a mecca for visitors. Aunt Jemima served them memorable meals. Her pancakes were famous as the "specialty of the house."

When the Mississippi side-wheeler, *Emily Dunstan*, caught fire near Higbee's Landing, Colonel Higbee opened his home to the survivors. Aunt Jemima's cheering words and stacks of her famous pancakes revived their spirits.

After the "War Between the States", a Confederate general recalled how he and his orderly stopped at Aunt Jemima's cabin to ask their way. She insisted they have a "snack" and served them pancakes the taste of which they never forgot.

Years later, a northern flour mill representative heard the story from the general while travelling down the river. At Higbee's Landing the two men went ashore to try to persuade Aunt Jemima to share her recipe with other homemakers.

The opportunity to make so many families happy with the ease and satisfaction of serving her mouth-watering pancakes was irresistible and Aunt Jemima left her cabin to begin her travels which have taken her up and down America.

Aunt Jemima made the first of her public appearances at the Columbian Exposition. Since then, millions of people have come to meet, know and love Aunt Jemima as a "real life" personality.

AUNT JEMIMA AT DISNEYLAND—When she's not lending a hand with Pancake Festivals, Aunt Jemima is "at home" in "Aunt Jemima's Kitchen" in Disneyland. In a gracious Old South setting, she welcomes you, serves her famous pancakes, and sends you on your way with a cheerful "You all come back!"

Free! 61 exciting ways to enjoy Aunt Jemima's Pancake Mix ...all in Magical Recipes booklet. Send request plus name and address to Quaker Oats Company, Sales Promotion Dept., Merchandise Mart Plaza, Chicago 11, Illinois.

Today Aunt Jemima's Community Pancake Days are raising millions of dollars for charities and civic projects and giving her friends the opportunity to meet and know Aunt Jemima in person.

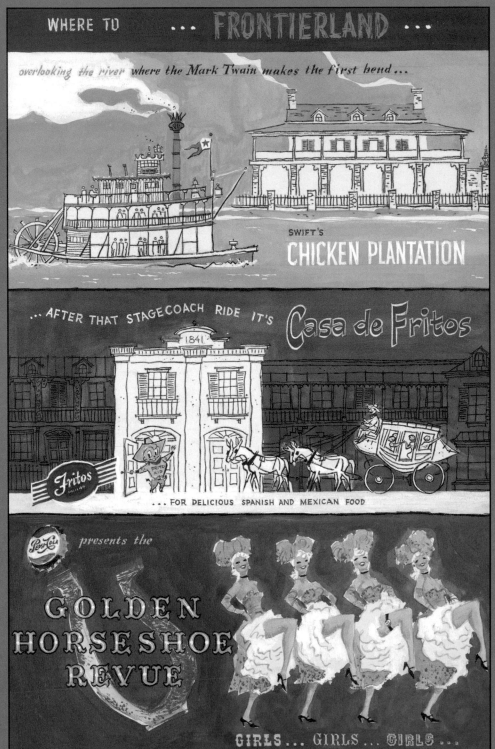

{TOP, LEFT} *Original location of Casa de Fritos, next to Aunt Jemima's Pancake House* • {ABOVE, LEFT} *Walt and Grandson Christopher on the terrace between Aunt Jemima's Pancake House and Casa de Fritos* • {ABOVE, RIGHT} *Frontierland restaurants poster by Sam McKim, 1956*

{OPPOSITE, TOP} *The Frito Kid concept art by Sam McKim, 1955* • {OPPOSITE, BOTTOM} *Casa de Fritos combination plate including Ta-cup on upper right of plate*

CASA DE FRITOS
AUGUST 11, 1955–CIRCA AUGUST 1966
ORIGINAL LOCATION
JULY 1, 1957–SEPTEMBER 1982
RELOCATED
*"For those who enjoy dining where 'different' foods
are available, Frontierland includes the Frito House,
where tacos and other Mexican foods are on the menu."*
—Disneyland News, September 1955

Mexican food was something of a novelty, even in California during the 1950s. The original 1955 Casa de Fritos location was next to Aunt Jemima's Pancake House. C. K. Doolin, the inventor of Fritos and owner of the company with the same name, was the lessee of the Tex-Mex restaurant, also known as the Frito House.

The Frito story started in 1932 when Doolin bought an original recipe for corn chips for one hundred dollars. Working in his mother's kitchen, he adapted the recipe, cutting the extruded dough into short thin ribbons, frying them in oil,

and salting them. He named the curved chips Fritos for "fried little things" and founded the Frito Company.

In the next decades Doolin went on to expand his empire with other snacks, including fried pork skins, roasted peanuts, peanut butter crackers, and potato chips. Doolin held many patents, including one for a fried tortilla basket, the "Ta-cup," which became a signature dish at Casa de Fritos. Doolin referred to it as an "open-face taco." He told the *Dallas Times Herald*, "You're supposed to eat a taco with your hands. Now it can be eaten like an open sandwich. The cup won't split and the customer doesn't get the filling all over himself." The filling was simple: ground hamburger, lettuce, shredded cheese, and red sauce. Other fare, supplied by Frito-owned Champion Foods, included tacos, tamales, and enchiladas, along with the more familiar chili and beans, spaghetti, and salads. Every order came with a bag of Fritos Corn Chips.

Despite all of Doolin's snack innovations, the invention of Doritos at Disneyland is attributed to a route salesman, not Doolin. Anaheim's Alex Foods Company supplied tortillas to Casa de Fritos. According to lore, one day the salesman noticed the cooks were throwing away stale tortillas and suggested they cut them into wedges and fry them instead. The impromptu tortilla chips were a hit and placed on the menu. Around 1961 Arch West, the marketing vice president of the newly merged Frito-Lay Company, noticed the popularity of the fried triangles. He contracted Alex Foods to manufacture them in bulk, purchasing all the required equipment. They were an instant hit when they were released nationally in 1966.

Despite Alex Foods' efforts to keep up with the demand, Frito-Lay took over and transferred production to their own plants in Birmingham, Alabama, and Tulsa, Oklahoma. The original Doritos were plain, without seasoning, which may explain why they were dubbed "little golden things" instead of "little orange things." (The taco flavor was added in 1967.)

The Frito Kid was the popular front man for Fritos; he was used in point-of-sale displays in supermarkets as early as 1937. Later, with a new and improved WED design, the mascot starred in an elaborate large and glassless "vending machine" located inside the Casa de Fritos restaurant. His cowboy costume is a nod to Doolin's Texas roots. Customers walked up to the ten-foot display and inserted a nickel. The life-sized blond Frito Kid would lick his lips, roll his eyes side to side, then sing a ditty such as, "Dig those chips, dig that gold, dig those chips of corn." Next his partner Klondike would chime in, "They are dark and salted too ... Fritos best for you" before the bag of corn chips would slide down the mine shaft. This is another example of Walt's way of engaging Disneyland Guests with food, helping them to anticipate it before they could eat it.

In March 1956, Case de Fritos asked Disneyland management for a larger location with more seating capacity. Soon thereafter the Frito House and the Frito Kid moved across Frontierland to a new building next to the Rainbow Caverns Mine Train (now Big Thunder Mountain Railroad). The restaurant reopened on July 1, 1957, on the occasion of Texas Day, with the Texas governor, Price Daniel, attending. Although Fritos' association with Disneyland ended in 1982, there's an homage of sorts to Casa de Fritos in the building it occupied, which is still a Mexican restaurant: just look behind the counter of the salad and dessert station. You'll see the framed California flag that flew outside the Frito House since dedication day in 1957.

DON DEFORE'S SILVER BANJO BARBECUE
June 15, 1957—March 4, 1962
"Where there is a rib, there is a relative."
—Don DeFore

Only one restaurant in the history of Disneyland displayed the name of someone other than Walt Disney (or one of his characters): Don DeFore's Silver Banjo Barbecue. The eponymous restaurant opened in 1957 and was owned by the television actor best known for portraying neighbor Thorny on *Ozzie and Harriet*.

The story begins in 1954, the same year *Disneyland* debuted. Walt had the idea to produce the prestigious Emmy Awards show for its first-ever national broadcast. But actor and Academy of Television Arts president Don DeFore was way ahead of him and arranged for the awards to be broadcast on NBC in 1955. Walt wasn't a sore loser. He invited Don to the studio; they toured the lot together and became fast friends. A few months later Don and his family were Walt's special guests on Disneyland's Opening Day.

Fast-forward to 1957. Casa de Fritos had moved across Frontierland and the small space adjacent to Aunt Jemima's Pancake House needed a new tenant. Coincidentally, Don was developing a restaurant concept of his own. He shared the story of his banjo-playing father and the resulting inspiration with the *Disneylander*:

> That well-loved and haunting sound of the silver banjo has never left me. And, what's more, I have ever since associated it with supper-time . . . and good food! A couple of years ago, while reminiscing with my younger brother Verne about those early childhood supper-time banjo fests, Verne mused, "Did you ever notice what a terrific appetite ya got from listening to that 'ol banjo strumming?"
>
> For two weeks, night and day, I worked on the idea and plans; and then, as if my Guardian Angel had been working with me, I heard that

there was going to be space available in Disneyland for someone to operate a barbecue restaurant. Negotiations were immediately started, and before long my brother Verne and I were welcomed into the Disneyland lessee family.

The "Guardian Angel" referred to was Bud Coulson, Disneyland's publicist and DeFore's former colleague at the Academy of Television. He recalled Don worked as a cook in college and invited him to try a new role as restaurateur. Although Don dabbled in his dorm kitchen, he was not a chef. Without a signature sauce of his own, he arranged to buy barbecue sauce from Loves, one of his favorite restaurants near his San Fernando Valley home in California.

In the first week of Silver Banjo's operation, the amount of sauce projected to last three days ran out in one. When it became obvious that Loves could not meet the demand, Don took a bottle of sauce to the UCLA chemistry lab for analysis. They were able to break down the recipe and identify ingredients, but not the exact quantities. Enter Don's wife, Marion DeFore. Working in her home kitchen, she blended and revised and taste-tested until she and her family agreed that she had hit upon a close version.

But that was only half the solution; she was in no position to make enough sauce in her home. Don sent the recipe to Hunt's to see if they could manufacture the sauce in quantity. They turned down the offer.

Ultimately, it wasn't the lack of a sauce manufacturer that plucked the final string on the Silver Banjo. After warnings from the city of Anaheim about inadequate facilities, Disneyland closed the Banjo to expand Aunt Jemima's kitchen. Don's career as a restaurateur may have ended; however, his television career was red hot. During the restaurant's last year, he was cast as boss man Mr. B on *Hazel*, with the fictional housekeeper of the same name doing all the cooking.

INDIAN VILLAGE JUICE BAR

The Indian Village was located on the far side of Frontierland and was the site of UPT's Indian Village Juice Bar. In 1962 they wanted to extend the menu and offer a selection of themed foods. Suggestions befitting the motif were sent to Disneyland's director of lessees, Jack Sayers, and included orange and grape "firewater," totem pole–shaped Sunkist frozen fruit bars, and corn on the cob.

OAKS TAVERN
1956–September 1978

The Oaks Tavern was right next door to The Golden Horseshoe. The simple offerings included hamburgers, cheeseburgers, chocolate brownies, and a choice of Pepsi or Coca-Cola.

In Walt's era there was also a Malt Shop, Cone Shop, and Fort Wilderness Snack Bar on Tom Sawyer Island.

For a brief time, Guests could fish in the Rivers of America. The practice was discontinued beacause the odors of the hours-old catch, wrapped in newspaper and carried from attraction to attraction, was not in keeping with Walt's mandate for a pristine park.

A Disneyland fun fact: one can identify the 1966 border between Frontierland and New Orleans Square by looking at the railing in front of the River Belle Terrace's patio seating. The Frontierland side has a wooden railing and the New Orleans Square side has wrought iron. A clay pot planted with rosemary sits between the two lands.

Chapter 6
WALT'S DISNEYLAND: FANTASYLAND

The Happiest Kingdom of them all. Here is the world of imagination, hopes, and dreams. In this timeless land of enchantment, the age of chivalry, magic, and make believe are reborn—and fairy tales come true. Fantasyland is dedicated to the young and the young at heart—to those who believe when you wish upon a star, your dreams do come true.
—WALT DISNEY, JULY 17, 1955

Fantasyland is all about make believe and the embodiment of Disney's full-length animated features. Of all the lands on Opening Day, Fantasyland had the most attractions, and almost all remain today, including Dumbo Flying Elephants, King Arthur Carrousel, Mad Tea Party, Mr. Toad's Wild Ride, Peter Pan's Flight, Casey Jr. Circus Train, and Snow White's Adventures.

The Fantasyland side of Sleeping Beauty Castle was originally designed as the front. However, Imagineer Herb Ryman didn't like it that way. Marty Sklar explains, "Herbie thought it should be reversed. One day he turned the model around, and at that moment Walt came in and said, "I like that better.""

Serendipity played its hand a second time in Fantasyland with "it's a small world." This time the Imagineer was Rolly Crump. He was getting his model ready for a meeting with Walt. All the trees were still on the roof of the model, waiting to be put on the ground where he designed them to be, when Walt walked in early and said, "Hey, that's a good idea." The trees remain today, albeit much larger, lending a unique dimension to the fabled attraction.

CHICKEN OF THE SEA PIRATE SHIP AND RESTAURANT
AUGUST 29, 1955–SEPTEMBER 1969
"The Pirate Ship offers proof that eating is fun at Disneyland."
—*Independent-Press-Telegram*, 1955

The Pirate Ship restaurant, sponsored by Chicken of the Sea, was situated in a lagoon in the back of Fantasyland where Dumbo flies today, in an area known as Pirate's Cove. It was a tribute to 1953's *Peter Pan*.

Canned tuna and tuna casseroles were staples of the mid-century American diet, making a tuna company the perfect corporate match for Walt's Pirate Ship Restaurant.

Beginning in 1954, StarKist and Chicken of the Sea were competing for the coveted sponsorship. In Chicken of the Sea's pitch, advertising manager Robert G. Dunham touted their brand icon: "Our little blond mermaid naturally fits into the character of Disneyland." He went on to emphasize that labels carrying their mermaid outsold every other brand in the country and their mermaid was "Disneyesque." (By 1961, StarKist had created Charlie Tuna to compete with her.)

Chicken of the Sea and their brand ambassador prevailed. After terms were reached, WED went to work on an intricately designed blond mermaid figurehead. It was modeled in clay, cast in plastic, and painted in full color at the Walt Disney Studios in Burbank before being mounted on the front of the ship serving as the restaurant.

Despite WED's best efforts, Fantasyland's flagship restaurant was only half-finished on Opening Day. The faithful re-creation of a Spanish man-of-war galleon, however, was open. As shown on the *Dateline Disneyland* television special, Guests traversed the seventy-five-foot-long gangway and explored from stem to stern. Six weeks later, food service below deck began. The predominantly seafood menu included oysters and shrimp, as well as salads, but the showstopper was the Tunaburger, essentially a warm tuna mixture with Thousand Island dressing and sweet pickles in a double-decker hamburger bun.

The number-one complaint at the Chicken of the Sea Pirate Ship was the coffee. It was not the thing to mess with at Disneyland. It was described in an internal memo as "the most putrid cup of coffee in the history of restaurant operation." The culprit was the vending machine that dispensed the coffee along with Coke, Pepsi, and orange soda; the remedy was a new service counter with dedicated coffee machines.

In its heyday, Disneyland's Pirate Ship Restaurant was one

of the most photographed restaurants in America. After it was dismantled, all was not destroyed. Salvaged lanterns, rigging, and bailing pins can be found in Peter Pan's Flight, including the ship's wheel, with Peter at the helm.

WELCH'S GRAPE JUICE BAR
JULY 24, 1955–1980

Welch's Grape Juice sponsored the *Mickey Mouse Club* television show in 1955, and as a result became one of Walt's lessees. The Welch's Grape Juice Bar was located between Snow White's Adventures and the Mickey Mouse Theater. The establishment sold grape juice, grape soda, grape sundaes, and Welchade, with an exclusive on all-grape beverages throughout the park.

There were two UPT-operated snack bars in Fantasyland. One was on the west side near the Skyway terminal, and the

other was on the east side next to Mr. Toad's Wild Ride.

The *Disneyland News* described the fare in an article: "Also feeding the Fantasyland famished are two snack and beverage stands, located on each side of the land. Hamburgers, hot dogs and ready sandwiches are here for those who wish to take as little time as possible from Fantasyland's rides and amusements."

Or as Card Walker instructed Jim Cora, a Disney Legend who worked his way up from Matterhorn host to chairman of Disneyland International, "Fantasyland will always be a hot dog and hamburger land."

CANDY KITCHEN
1957–CIRCA 1968

The Candy Kitchen was a smaller outpost for A. R. Brooks Corporation, the operators of the Candy Palace on Main Street, U.S.A. It was located on the east side of Sleeping Beauty Castle.

THE MATTERHORN AND SWISS CHEESE

When asked why there were holes in the Matterhorn, Walt was known to smile and reply, "Because it's a Swiss mountain." All jokes aside, the assignment for the world's first double tubular steel track was a tough one for Bob Gurr, who said, "It's a roller coaster inside a cone; the track was hidden inside, and it had to be designed around the holes for the Skyway buckets."

With necessity being the mother of invention, Gurr was game and later said, "There was no criteria. I just kept trying to make it work." In the end, the Tomorrowland side of the attraction's track is steeper and with a tighter radius. As a result, it's a slightly longer and faster ride there than on the Fantasyland side.

{ABOVE} *Nautical figurehead for the Pirate Ship Restaurant—while it was still under construction—awaits installation on a Disney studio soundstage.*

Chapter 7
WALT'S DISNEYLAND:
TOMORROWLAND

A vista into a world of wondrous ideas, signifying man's achievements . . .
a step into the future, with the predictions of constructive things to come.
Tomorrow offers new frontiers in science, adventure, and ideals: the Atomic Age . . .
the challenge of outer space . . . and the hope for a peaceful and unified world.
—Walt Disney, July 17, 1955

He was really into Tomorrowland.
—Diane Disney Miller

Tomorrowland's futuristic theme was set in 1986, the year Haley's Comet would return to Earth—the farthest Imagineers could fathom. Walt wanted to carry the theme of Tomorrowland to the letter, even if it was daunting. "Tomorrow is a heck of a thing to keep up with," he quipped.

The Imagineers had run out of time and funds to finish Tomorrowland before Disneyland opened on July 17, 1955. Marty Sklar noted, "So much was thrown together to fill the spaces." That included the sets from 1954's *Twenty Thousand Leagues Under the Sea*—ironic, since the film is set in 1886, one hundred years earlier than the time frame of this land. Crane's "Bathroom of the Future" displayed designer fixtures and forward-thinking home bathroom concepts such as telephones near toilets and dumbbells for bathtub workouts. Fiberglass chairs, with a table attached on the side and a cup holder conveniently built in, were placed not only at restaurants, but throughout the land, also to fill the void. The Kaiser Aluminum Pig, affectionately known as KAP, also fit that bill. KAP was the mascot for Kaiser Aluminum (unprocessed aluminum is known as "pig"). The small exhibit extolled the virtues of aluminum and how Americans couldn't live without it—from giant jet airplanes to small pots and pans—and featured a giant walk-in aluminum telescope.

SPACE BAR
JULY 17, 1955–SEPTEMBER 5, 1966 AND 1967–1977

There was only one restaurant in Tomorrowland on Opening Day: the Space Bar, operated by UPT, was intended to be a sneak preview of the future of food. A small walk-up grill served hamburgers, hot dogs, tuna sandwiches, and pie. There were a few modernistic vending machines that delivered food at the push of a button, and although that was somewhat thrilling in 1955, the Space Bar was a downsized version of the futuristic and fully automated Automat that was conceived but never built.

It was here that chewing gum, banned by Walt to keep his park immaculate, was briefly sold undetected. Jim Cora recalls him saying, "When you see my movies in theaters, and there is gum on the seat, it's not my fault. But when you go to Disneyland, it is my fault." Sales were discontinued immediately after the sticky situation was discovered.

Autopia, a few steps from the Space Bar, represented "The Freeway of the Future." Guests seven and above (before height requirements) would get licensed before heading onto the road in a "car of tomorrow"—without a guide track! (It took several years before they installed one.) Safety measures included a top speed of eleven miles an hour, a single pedal that would engage the braking mechanism when released, and lap belts, a standard in the amusement industry even though seat belts didn't become mandatory in California until 1986. Walt had his own custom car painted metallic maroon, with a red and off-white interior. He delighted in being in the passenger seat with one of his grandchildren at the wheel.

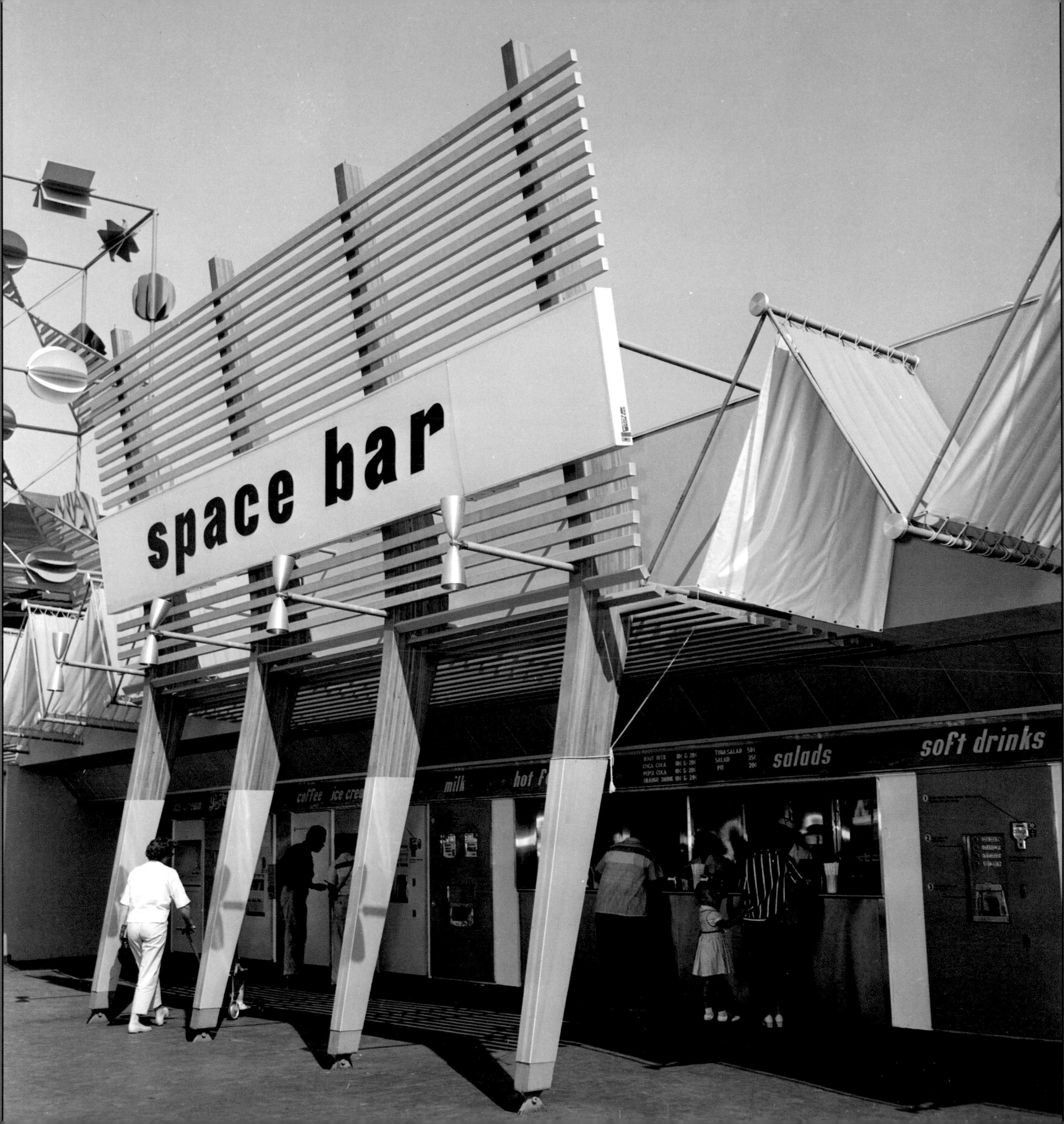
space bar
coffee
milk
salads
soft drinks

THE YACHT CLUB
Summer 1955–September 6, 1966
Renamed and Relocated 1957
THE YACHT BAR
1957–1966

The Yacht Club followed later in the summer, overlooking the Phantom Boats attraction on the banks of the Tomorrowland Lagoon, thus the nautical name. The small boats with the big fins had skippers operating outboard motors from the rear, later replaced with boats Guests could "steer" themselves on underwater tracks. The fare was more of the same: hamburgers, cheeseburgers, hot dogs, French fries, pizza, and the marine-themed submarine sandwiches.

In 1957, the Yacht Club moved near the Matterhorn Bobsleds to make room for the Viewliner attraction. Renamed the Yacht Bar, it remained at that location until it sailed into the sunset during the Tomorrowland remodel.

Even though the ice cream wagons in Tomorrowland were operated by UPT, their design was overseen and approved by

WED. In 1957, Disney Legend Richard "Dick" Irvine, one of the key art directors for Disneyland, was very specific with UPT's Frank Stabile: "The body of the cart should be painted as suggested in sketch #1, with the Tomorrowland yellow and persimmon. This color should be checked out with John Hench. The top of the wagon could be in stainless steel and the hood on sketch #1 could be made of stainless. If you prefer the umbrella on sketch #2, this would be of canvas and similar to the umbrellas that they use in the patio of the Disneyland Hotel. Canvas could be in the same color scheme as the cart. The push bar would also be of stainless and could be designed in several ways as indicated, the selection to be determined by you based on cost. We would like to see the revised sketch before you order them."

DAIRY BAR
January 21, 1956–September 1, 1958
"Today's Food Builds Tomorrow's Man."

The Dairy Association's snack stand was an ultramodern dairy bar and very popular. It sold milk shakes, malts, ice cream, and plain milk until an exclusive contract with Carnation to provide milk products throughout the park forced the association's exit.

The imagined exhibit, never realized, was for the Cow of the Future—Bossy. She would live with other plastic demonstration cows in air-conditioned stalls, with televisions broadcasting images of rolling green hills. The herd would eat "scientifically controlled food," living under large lamps to kill germs and build vitamin D. The Cows of the Future would be milked by an automated machine, with their milk analyzed for butterfat, protein, and carbohydrates. The Milkman of Tomorrow would receive the milk through a pipeline, ultimately delivering it in bottles via a "single unit helicopter."

How would Walt, who said Tomorrowland was "a step into the future with predictions of constructive things to come," have reacted to twenty-first-century realities so close to this vision, like home deliveries via drones?

MONSANTO HOUSE OF THE FUTURE
June 1957–December 1967
"This kitchen almost gets dinner itself, but that wouldn't really be fun. The fun is making the most of the ultimate in kitchen convenience and efficiency. The dream of the future brought to reality by Monsanto."

The Monsanto House of the Future, built almost entirely in plastic, was a walk-through attraction that featured a kitchen with appliances virtually unheard of at the time, including an ultrasonic dishwasher that doubled as a cupboard and what is believed to be the first compact microwave in America. Instead of a traditional refrigerator and freezer, there were cold zones that lowered electrically from an overhead cabinet. The Crane Climate Control system allowed the air-conditioning—with scents if desired—to be controlled by the push of a button in the kitchen. Walt teased Diane it would be the perfect home for her growing family.

THE POPCORN PEOPLE

You may have walked past the carts, even ordered popcorn without noticing the tiny characters that are rotating the canisters attached to a faux steam pump. They're "toastie-roasties" (originally named "Tosty Rosty" by the Cretor Company, the inventor of the original popcorn machines used at Disneyland) and are themed to the land in which they perform. You will find a spaceman in Tomorrowland, a nod to the walk-around character of Walt's era, and an Abominable Snowman (something Walt always intended for the Matterhorn)—he has a name—Harold—and resides near the bobsleds. Finding the rest is up to you; I don't want to spoil the fun.

HOW LUNCH LED TO ONE OF THE MOST FAMOUS DISNEYLAND PHOTOS EVER

Imagineer and Disney Legend Tony Baxter shared an "unknown food story" told to him by Wendell "Bud" Hurlbut. The year was 1959. Walt was reimagining all of Tomorrowland, including three new attractions—the Matterhorn, Submarine Voyage, and the Monorail. Bud was designing and building the Calico Mine Ride at Knott's Berry Farm with a significant budget. Walt had visited Bud's kiddie parks years before, sitting and observing as he liked to do, even consulting with Bud on the layout of Disneyland; Bud went on to build the King Arthur Carrousel in Fantasyland. They were friends that shared a love of amusement parks and trains. After Walt checked out the progress on the subs, he would stop by to see Bud and his dark ride under construction. Afterward they would have lunch. Walt liked the food at Knott's chicken restaurant; however, he was so recognizable in the park he couldn't enjoy his meals there. That prompted

Bud to find local places that catered to Walt's simple tastes. Bud told Tony, "My circle was getting larger and larger because I used up all the things that Walt loved. He really took enjoyment in going to a different restaurant every time he came to the area because it was an area he wasn't familiar with. We finally got from Buena Park all the way up to Whittier and a restaurant called Nixon's."

Nixon's was owned by Donald Nixon, the brother of Richard Nixon. Walt ordered the coffee shop's homemade bean soup and was an instant fan. So much so that Bud recounted to Tony, "It was curious. Like a person who had been in the Depression or something. He'd get to the bottom of the bowl and he'd grab the bread and start wiping the bowl. It was ready to go back on the shelf it was that clean when he was finished."

The second time they went, Walt set out to meet Don Nixon. He really liked the food, but he had another agenda. "I love your bean soup. Everything is great. By the way, is there any chance you can talk your brother into opening my Monorail?" Apparently the tactic worked. Vice President Richard Nixon and his wife, Pat, presided over the ceremony. Their daughters, Julie and Tricia, had the honor of cutting the ribbon. Unfortunately, it turned out to be an honorary role: the scissors were too dull to cut through. An experienced showman, Walt stepped in and ripped the ribbon, and the Monorail was officially opened.

Tony wraps it up neatly: "The whole Disneyland fifty-nine with the photo of Walt and Nixon cutting the ribbon happened because Bud Hurlbut took Walt to Donald Nixon's restaurant in Whittier. It was all because of food."

{OPPOSITE} *Photo taken at the official opening (not the staged one from earlier in the day for the press). Fun fact: one can distinguish Disneyland's staged photos versus those taken at an actual event by looking for people in the park.*

WALT DISNEY

May 8, 1959.

MAY 1 1 1959

Dear Dick Nixon -

Your brother, Don, has informed me that you intend to be here with your family around the middle of June. We would like to take this opportunity to invite you, your family and your mother to be our honored guests on the occasion of the inaugural ceremonies dedicating the start of our fifth year at Disneyland when we will introduce some new and fascinating attractions.

Among these is a replica of the famed Matterhorn, complete with bobsled rides; an adventure with a fleet of eight atomic submarines taking people under water to the world of liquid space and two Alweg Monorail Trains which are a prototype of a rapid transit system which may solve many of the traffic problems of our modern day.

There will also be a parade on Sunday the 14th, starting in the afternoon.

ABC will make a live telecast of the entire ceremonies which will be aired on Monday the 15th.

It would be wonderful if you and your family could be with us and stay at the Disneyland Hotel Saturday night, and Sunday if you can spare the time. I have gone ahead and reserved Jack Wrather's personal suite (Jack is the owner of the hotel) for you and your family, as well as space for your mother. There will also be rooms for the Secret Service Men.

Your presence here would make our opening a memorable event for everyone and I sincerely hope it will be possible for you to attend.

With my kindest regards and best wishes,

Sincerely,

Walt Disney

The Honorable Richard M. Nixon,
Vice President of the United States,
Senate Office Building,
Washington, D.C.

Chapter 8
WALT'S LAST LAND: NEW ORLEANS SQUARE

Disneyland has always had a big river and a Mississippi stern-wheeler.
It seemed appropriate to create a new attraction at the bend of the river.
And so Disneyland's New Orleans Square came into being: a New Orleans
of a century ago when she was the 'Gay Paree' of the American frontier.
—WALT DISNEY

{RIGHT} *New Orleans Square, concept art by Herb Ryman, 1964*

New Orleans Square, a tribute to the Crescent City, was the last major land overseen by Walt. He dedicated it on July 24, 1966, along with the mayor of the real New Orleans, Victor Hugo "Vic" Shiro. (There was a small kerfuffle when Walt suggested his land was cleaner than the mayor's city.) Notably, it's the only land in the Magic Kingdom that debuted without attractions—Pirates of the Caribbean was still under construction. The adjacent Blue Bayou Restaurant was ready for business; however, Walt wouldn't allow it to open without the swashbuckling spectacle ferrying Guests in operation. "It's a bad show to look out at the bayou without pirate boats floating by," Walt lamented.

Pirates of the Caribbean was originally conceived as a walk-through attraction and wax museum. However, because of concerns over guest flow and capacity, it was reimagined as a boat ride similar to it's a small world and to showcase the Audio-Animatronics perfected for the 1964–65 New York World's Fair just a few years earlier.

Imagineer and Disney Legend Francis Xavier "X" Atencio wrote the sixteen-minute script for the attraction. Some of his colleagues were concerned that it was too long, but Walt

disagreed: "It's like a cocktail party: you hear bits and pieces of conversation, and you get the idea of what's going on. Our boat ride is even better; if you want to hear the rest of the conversation, come back for another ride!"

Walt passed away four months before Pirates of the Caribbean opened in March of 1967. Sadly, he never raised a glass or unfolded a napkin at any of the New Orleans Square restaurants he championed—Blue Bayou, Creole Café, and the private Club 33.

BLUE BAYOU RESTAURANT
MARCH 18, 1967–PRESENT

"Here on the Blue Bayou Terrace, as you enjoy fine cuisine, you may re-live one of these worlds—the mysterious water wonderland of the Bayous. Here where Spanish moss drapes the live oak trees, where shrimp boats hide amongst the cypress, where a waterfront shanty stands in the shadow of a graceful plantation mansion—here are the strange sounds and marvelous sights of the Louisiana bayou."—1966 brochure text

Blue Bayou—the name won out over Le Restaurant de Blue Mystique and Terrace de Blue Bayou—exemplifies themed-dining experiences and is still considered a prototype for the industry. As early as June 1961, Walt and his Imagineers were discussing entertainment concepts for the restaurant situated in eternal moonlight.

Atencio, who composed the iconic "Yo Ho (A Pirate's Life for Me)," proposed a musical number blending the bayou's natural sounds and traditional New Orleans jazz instrumentation. "[I heard] the croaking of a frog, joined by the chirping of a cricket to start the beat," he said. "Other creatures such as birds and animals and an occasional musical instrument could join in to develop the beat until a swinging melody is achieved."

{OPPOSITE} *Blue Bayou in 1967, with Walt's artist Charles Boyer cast as a diner at center back table, second from left*

melody is achieved." Although several versions of the theme were recorded, none of them were ever used. The crickets and frogs, however, were cast in the background.

It was following a preview audience that Walt emphatically decided there would be no entertainment as originally planned: "In this restaurant the food is going to be the show, along with the atmosphere."

Walt wanted to honor the French and Spanish culinary traditions of New Orleans. Blue Bayou showcases Creole and Cajun specialties, but the Monte Cristo sandwich was the star. While the sandwich may not be authentic to the Crescent City—it's a cousin to France's Croque Monsieur and believed to have originated in Southern California—it remains one of the most popular menu items at Disneyland.

Blue Bayou was the first reservation-based eatery at Disneyland. However, a table couldn't be secured by telephone. Once the park opened, Guests had to physically go to the restaurant to sign up for an available time, often prompting a mad dash as soon as the gates opened. Today reservations may be made up to sixty days in advance through Disney Dining.

CLUB 33
JUNE 15, 1967–PRESENT
"Walt Disney's concept—an elegant, exclusive club for Very Important People . . . a place for conversation, and in turn a conversation piece in its own right."
—1967 Club 33 sales brochure

There was one building under construction in New Orleans Square that wasn't intended for the public—the Disney family apartment above Pirates of the Caribbean. Disney Legend Dorothea Redmond, who collaborated with Alfred Hitchcock before coming to WED in 1964, painted exquisite watercolor renderings for Walt. Emile Kuri, who decorated

the apartment above the firehouse, traveled with Walt and Lillian to New Orleans to select antiques for "The Royal Suite," once again theming the decor to be consistent with its land. Although it was close to completion in 1966, Roy halted construction after his brother died, saying it would be too sad for the family to ever use it.

One element of the era, however, remains: the "W" and "R" cast in wrought iron on the second-floor veranda, the spot where Walt would have had a bird's-eye view of the Rivers of America, Tom Sawyer Island, his sailing ships, and the bustle of New Orleans below.

A commercial kitchen was built next to the apartment with a dual purpose—for the family's chef and for the adjacent restaurant and private club, where Walt planned to entertain potential Walt Disney World investors and VIPs. The executive lounge at the 1964–65 World's Fair was one of his inspirations. So was the 21 Club in New York City, and interestingly, when the articles of incorporation were filed with the Secretary of State of California, it was listed as "33 Club." Jim Cora recalls that RETLAW employees (*Walter* spelled backwards and the name of the company that oversaw Walt's personal holdings, including the two attractions he owned—the trains and Monorail) were told thirty-three symbolized the number of sponsors and lessees at the time of New Orleans Square's dedication.

While that turns out to be accurate accounting, the enigma surrounding Club 33's name prevails. Thirty-three didn't represent the number of Imagineers who created Disneyland, nor the amount of original lessees. And even though Club 33 is the only place in Disneyland that serves alcohol, an idea Walt initially rejected, the Club wasn't assigned an address (there weren't many outside Main Street, U.S.A.)—and thus the name—to obtain a liquor license.

Grandson Walter Miller, however, may have come upon

the keenest theory: No. 33 is in honor of Diane Disney Miller's birth year.

This author wonders why it wasn't named Club 13. Even though superstitious folks are averse to the number, I believe that thirteen was Walt's favorite number: Walt was married on July 13. The Carolwood caboose at his home was numbered thirteen. Lillian's license plate was LBD13 [Lillian Bounds Disney]. There were thirteen original colonies in America, the country Walt loved fiercely. "If you could see close in my eyes, the American flag is waving in both of them, and up my spine is growing this red, white, and blue stripe." Disneyland's address is 1313 Harbor Boulevard (and it's believed to have been hand-selected), all because the thirteenth letter in the alphabet is M—as in Mickey Mouse.

Club 33's initial membership consisted mostly of Disneyland's corporate partners and Orange County, California, busi-

{ABOVE} *Club 33's main dining room*

Club 33, Royal Street, New Orleans Square,

1313 HARBOR BOULEVARD, ANAHEIM, CALIFORNIA 92803   TELEPHONE (714) 533-4533

DISNEYLAND

Walt Disney's Magic Kingdom

CHILDREN'S DINNER

Club 33

California Fruit Cup, Supreme
or
Tomato Juice

Soup du jour   or   Tossed Green Salad

CHOICE OF

Ground Sirloin of Beef, Mushroom Sauce
Fried Chicken with Country Gravy
Baked Virginia Ham, Bing Cherry Sauce
Roast Beef au jus

WITH

Vegetable   Potato
Roll and Butter

CHOICE OF

Blackbeard Sundae   Mary Poppins Sundae
French Pastry   Chocolate Pudding

Beverage

$2.00

{OPPOSITE} *Club 33 foyer concept art by S Carpenter, 1965* • {THIS PAGE} *Club 33 Menu, 1967*

nessmen. The entrance was discreet, blending into the facade next to the Blue Bayou with only a small 33 to distinguish it. Members would press a small, nondescript brass button and when granted admission after communicating through an intercom, the door would magically slide open.

The Banquet Room and the Trophy Room were the two main dining areas, along with the Lounge Alley, which housed the bar and buffet. The formal banquet room was resplendent in nineteenth-century French style decor. The Trophy Room, with its masculine motif, was planned as Walt's personal space. Hunting trophies provided by Walt's friends and Audio-Animatronics contributed by the Imagineers were mounted on the walls. Microphones were hidden in the chandeliers, placed there with Walt's playful intention to interact and improvise with his guests.

The idea was basic magic: an actor would sit in an adjacent room, listen to the conversation, and respond as the voice of the vulture. Although the show never went on in Walt's lifetime, the feathered predator remains perched in the club.

Club 33 is a "private show within a public show." Amid the casual eateries and popcorn wagons exists a gourmet restaurant with fine linen and china, white tablecloth service, and no paper napkins. The fare in Walt's era was what was known then as Continental, largely French along with classic American preparations. Buffets and menu service were both offered at Club 33. The wine list was impressive, with imported selections from Château Margaux, included for its prestige even if too expensive for most Guests, to California brands, including Wente Bros. and Buena Vista. A separate menu provided Guests with suggested wine and food pairings. The dress code was fairly strict, though it was unlikely, no matter how formal the setting, a Guest would be asked to remove his Mouse Ears.

Club 33 remains in its original second-floor location; however, the entrance has been moved down to 33 Orleans Street.

CREOLE CAFÉ
1966–Present

Coffee came to America by way of New Orleans in the mid-1700s. The city is known for its strong coffee, and Walt's New Orleans Square wouldn't be complete without a coffeehouse of its own. And Creole Café is just that, with coffee specialties beyond the basic black, and French-inspired snacks/delicacies, including croissants, petit fours, napoleons, and éclairs. The Patisserie Francois Café and Bourbon Street Coffee House were names that were bantered about. Animator, Imagineering show designer, and Disney Legend Marc Davis used the name Coffee Call on one of his set renderings. However, it was dubbed Creole Café and later changed to Café Orleans.

Chapter 9
OSCAR AND INDIAN

Get along with everybody, and if you smile, you make friends.
—Oscar's recipe for success

Never stop learning, and always try to do better.
—Indian's recipe for success

This wouldn't be a book about the culinary history of Disneyland without mentioning two beloved and respected chefs during Walt's era and beyond.

Oscar is Disneyland's longest-serving employee, and thus a legend. Raised on a farm in Arkansas, he came to Anaheim at his girlfriend Shirley's behest. She was already a Disneyland employee when Oscar was hired at age twenty-one on December 29, 1956. His first job was working as a busboy at the Fantasyland 1 and 2 snack stands. "We had about ten people working there. They said, 'Here is the orange juice and here is the grape.' That was about all the training I had," he remembers. Later he became a grill cook at both locations.

Oscar was timid and did not speak unless spoken to. When he was asked to deliver milk from Fantasyland to Tomorrowland, he hand-carried each and every case. His supervisor was impressed by the effort, yet wondered why he didn't use a dolly. For Oscar it was obvious: "I was too shy to ask for one."

After the brief stint in Fantasyland, a short time spent flipping hamburgers at the Space Bar in Tomorrowland, and jobs at Plaza Gardens and Hills Bros., Oscar spent most of his career at the Carnation Café.

Shirley, whom he married after coming to California, had the distinction of being the person who made Walt's milk shakes. "She used to make them just the way he liked them. A combination of chocolate and vanilla ice cream, with chocolate syrup. He liked them with not too much ice cream and not too much milk. Walt came by once when she had the day off and he wasn't very happy with how they made the shake that day."

Oscar never met Walt personally nor cooked for him. However, he recalls that whenever "Mr. Walt" ate at the Carnation Café, he liked to sit by himself in the back. Oscar recalls that employees were instructed not to approach him, as he appreciated his anonymity. "He liked to see how people reacted to the place." Early in the morning, before the park opened, Oscar would frequently see him sitting alone on a bench on Main Street. "He had this little book. He would keep track of everything and he wanted it to be just right." It's this pursuit of perfection that continues to influence Oscar's style. "I run this place the way Walt Disney would want it."

In the 1960s, Oscar was also renowned for his off-menu, Cast-Members–only chorizo and eggs. "He was the only one who could make it right," according to Jim Cora. "Others tried, but it was never the same."

One afternoon, standing outside the Carnation Café, Oscar was willing to share his recipe. In his already quiet voice, he whispered, "The secret is in the technique. Cook the chorizo in a double boiler, let the sausage cook gently." He paused briefly, reflecting back on the decades since he's prepared it.

"Drain the chorizo on paper towels and pat it dry to get the extra grease out," he advised. "In a skillet with melted butter, scramble the eggs with the chorizo. You can add cooked diced potatoes if you want. Season with salt and pepper. You must always taste it before you serve it!"

Duly noted—he's serious about this. In the ten minutes since we first huddled, the line of fans waiting for a hug and a photo had grown. Before posing with his public, he whispered, "Put the eggs in a warm tortilla with hot sauce and guacamole. That's how you do it."

Tony Baxter and Oscar share a bond from the 1960s that continues today. "Oscar was my first lead. I always acknowledged him because when you are seventeen years old, you are looking for someone who is nice and nonthreatening and taking you under his wing. And that was Oscar."

The mutual affection is obvious. "I always knew Tony was special and smart. When he showed me his drawings for the *Mary Poppins* attraction, I told him how good he was.

I encouraged him to do more than ice cream," recalls Oscar.

"A lot of people, I think they want something special from me, with my name on it." And while there was an Oscar Salad years ago, something he'd love to bring back for lunch or dinner, one tribute remains on the Carnation Café menu: Oscar's Choice. The typical American breakfast features eggs, bacon or sausage, toast and Oscar's signature potatoes—the menu item that first got him noticed. Oscar explains, "You have to stay with the potatoes. You can't walk away. They need to be basted with butter every five minutes."

Oscar works the early shift, arriving in the morning before the restaurant begins service. When the gates open, Oscar steps outside and waves to the Guests on Main Street. It's more than a ritual. It's part of Oscar's business. "When the Guests see me, the place fills up."

HIDEO "INDIAN" ARAMAKI

Hideo "Indian" Aramaki began his career at the Tahitian Terrace in 1964. "I took a cut in pay, but when I saw the cleanliness of the kitchen, the equipment and the way things were run, I was happy."

Hideo did not have any formal culinary training. After he graduated high school he worked in the sugarcane fields of Maui, Hawaii, to help support his family. By the time he was twenty in 1935, Hideo was playing semiprofessional baseball for the Cleveland Indians. It was there his childhood nickname, Indian, given to him by boyhood buddies in his hometown of Puuenne, Hawaii, stuck forever.

After a brief internment during World War II in Arizona, Indian began cooking in Chicago. "Imagine a Japanese-named Indian starting a Jewish-Chinese restaurant on Chicago's South Side. I didn't know anything about cooking, but my wife did." Indian was a quick learner and soon became an accomplished chef himself. That led to eight years at a restaurant in Santa Ana, California, and then Disneyland.

Unlike Oscar, who never met Walt personally, Indian did. "In my early days as a chef's assistant at the Plaza Pavilion, I would see Walt Disney every Sunday morning in the park before [its] opening. One day he heard someone calling me Indian and he said, 'If that's what everyone calls you, why don't you get it on your name tag?'" This was an exception for Walt and one of the few times he allowed an employee to have a nickname on their name tag.

Indian prided himself on keeping his eyes on the bottom line. "I was boasting to Walt Disney one morning about the low food costs and high profit rate, and Walt stopped me and said, 'Indian, just make sure you serve our Guests good food and don't worry so much about costs.'" As such, even though food at Disneyland was cooked in mass quantities, Indian never allowed compromise. "Simple, good food cooked and served right. That's the main thing."

During his tenure he was instrumental in the opening of Club 33 and had the honor of cooking for several dignitaries, including Emperor Hirohito and Empress Nagako of Japan. But his biggest claim to fame may be putting the Monte Cristo sandwich on the Blue Bayou menu. "Indian was the kindest, most respected man. One heck of an administrator," recalls Jim Hilinski, director of construction contract administration and purchasing for Disneyland and Indian's close friend. "He was a gracious host but a stickler for procedure and he enforced it greatly. People enjoyed working with him." He had a commanding presence. Imagineer Kevin Rafferty, who worked for Indian as a busser at the Plaza Inn, says, "He was large and in charge."

In 1966 Indian was promoted to executive chef for all of Disneyland's food establishments, including the Disneyland Hotel. He held that position until his retirement in 1985.

Chapter 10
DINING OUTSIDE DISNEYLAND: WALT'S FAVORITE RESTAURANTS

There were a lot of iceberg lettuce salads with blue cheese dressing when we went out to eat.
—Jenny, Walt's Granddaughter

BUSINESS LUNCHES

Walt ate lunch off the lot, too. Among the restaurants he frequented between 1934 and 1966 were Romanoff's, Chasen's, Barclay Kitchen, Brown Derby, and Perino's (all closed).

Walt also ate in hotel restaurants, including the Biltmore, Beverly Hills Hotel, Beverly Hilton, and Beverly Wilshire (all still open).

SMOKE TREE RANCH
1850 Smoke Tree Lane, Palm Springs, California

One of the favorite places to eat as a family was in the resort community of Palm Springs. Walt and Lillian had a second home at Smoke Tree Ranch where everyone liked to gather. Jenny recalls that her grandpa "was always present when we were there . . . listening to us, enjoying us, and watching us."

Walt was an avid lawn bowler and was known to dress the part in all-white attire. He was also an accomplished equestrian. Besides polo, he liked morning trail rides followed by an outdoor picnic of scrambled eggs and pancakes cooked in cast iron skillets.

There is Disneyland history to be learned from the resort: Walt sold his first home, designed by William Cody, to help with the down payment on his Magic Kingdom. (He built another home in 1957, but because of strict architectural regulations, was not allowed to run a small railroad around the house; the track's footprint became a paved path for the grandkids' bikes.)

Walt offered Disneyland investment opportunities to his fellow members, known as "Colonists." However, they all declined. His ties, embroidered with the Smoke Tree Ranch logo, could be seen on episodes of *Disneyland* and *Walt Disney's Wonderful World of Color*, although most viewers would not have known the significance of the insignia. Those ties were so special to Walt—along with the fond memories at Smoke Tree Ranch—that he's wearing one on the *Partners* statue in the hub of Disneyland and the other Disney Parks around the world.

CHASEN'S AND HERNANDO'S HIDEAWAY
Both Closed

Walt didn't venture out to the swanky Hollywood hot spots often, but when he did, he preferred Chasen's, for the chili, and Hernando's Hideaway, where good old-fashioned food was served, along with Mexican fare.

TAM O'SHANTER
2980 Los Feliz Boulevard, Los Angeles, California

About forty-five minutes north of Disneyland sits Tam O' Shanter. Established in 1922, it remains the oldest restaurant in Los Angeles owned by the same family in the same location. Its fairy-tale exterior, resembling the old Normandy region, is thought to be one of the many inspirations for Snow White's house.

During the late 1920s and throughout the 1930s (the Hyperion Studio days with no on-site cafeteria), Walt and his staff ate lunch there so often it was referred to as the "Disney Commissary." It was so often that Walt knew every busboy by name. The food was in Walt's wheelhouse, including "Hamburger Sandwiches" made with freshly ground hamburger and served on a buttered and grilled piece of white bread instead of a bun.

The legend is that Walt's table is number thirty-one. It's a nice corner table with four chairs, however Tony Baxter confirms that the booth where Walt ate and worked with his trusted animators and story men is number thirty-five. The pegs that held hats—or a curtain when privacy was needed—are still there today. And table thirty-one? Consider it a tribute table designed by Imagineering, with doodles representing some of WED's futuristic plans from the 1960s, created to please the fans still flocking to the Tam.

The influence the restaurant had on Disneyland is twofold: the Tam's servers wear tartan plaid, just like the VIP guides at Disneyland, although it was Lillian who chose the Royal

Stewart pattern for the park. And the restaurant's proprietor, Richard Frank, was one of Walt's consultants for the park's "Feeding Operations" in the early 1950s.

Tam O'Shanter serves lunch and dinner seven days a week. Check the reception area for the two pieces of art that reflect Walt's admiration of the restaurant and its multigenerational owners, including one drawn by John Hench.

BIFF'S
Closed, Los Angeles

Walt enjoyed the breakfast at Biff's. His usual order was the silver dollar pancakes; however, he was also a fan of their pan-fried potatoes, which he declared were "done right." He liked them so much he instructed Thelma to keep going back to the restaurant until she could duplicate them. She completed her assignment, reporting that they were actually hash-browned (smaller pieces of potato and crispier) and not pan-fried (chunks of potatoes cooked more softly with onions and peppers), but Walt didn't care what they were called. He wanted Biff's-style breakfast potatoes at home, and he got them.

CLIFTON'S CAFETERIA
648 S Broadway, Los Angeles, California

Clifton's Cafeteria, a portmanteau of its founder's first and last names, was established during the Depression in 1931 by Clifford Clinton. Clinton was a devout Christian and he installed a flashing neon sign outside the restaurant that read PAY WHAT YOU WISH. Inside it was kitschy, with a forest-themed decor that included towering redwood trees. After a trip to the South Seas, Clinton introduced a tropical jungle theme, which included a Polynesian grass hut and a rain effect that went off every twenty minutes. Some historians believe the restaurant may have inspired Walt during the development of Disneyland, his Enchanted Tiki Room in particular, even before his own trip to the South Seas in 1934.

Another fascinating parallel between Clifton's Cafeteria and Disneyland are the enveloping and carefree experiences they provided to their guests. Clifton's billed itself as "[a] theme park restaurant of imagination, dreams[,] and whimsy—away from the troubles that we hope can be left at the door for just a little while."

MONTY'S STEAKHOUSE
5371 Topanga Canyon Boulevard, Woodland Hills, California (Encino, California, location where Walt ate has closed.)

Meals at this upscale chain restaurant were a favorite of the Miller and Disney families. Walt particularly liked a wedge salad with iceberg lettuce and blue cheese dressing.

SMOKE HOUSE
4420 Lakeside Drive, Burbank, California

This restaurant is close to all the neighboring studios. Everyone from executives to stars to stagehands enjoyed the clubhouse atmosphere. Celebrities—like Walt and Clark Gable—could eat in peace, as the patrons' privacy was respected.

PINK'S HOT DOGS
709 North La Brea Avenue, Los Angeles, California

Walt came to this iconic Los Angeles stand, established in 1939, on the corner of Melrose and La Brea, for two things: a plain hot dog and a strawberry soda.

MARTINO'S ORIGINAL BAKERY
335 North Victory Boulevard, Burbank, California (new location, post-Walt)

Established in 1926, Martino's began supplying tea cakes for the Inking & Painting Tea Lounge at the Walt Disney Studios beginning in 1940. Although ownership has changed over the years, the secret tea cake recipe has not. The bakery in Burbank is open six days a week.

"To all who come to this happy place: Welcome. Disneyland is your land."

—Walt Disney

{RIGHT} *Disneyland map (including future planned attractions) by Sam McKim, 1958*

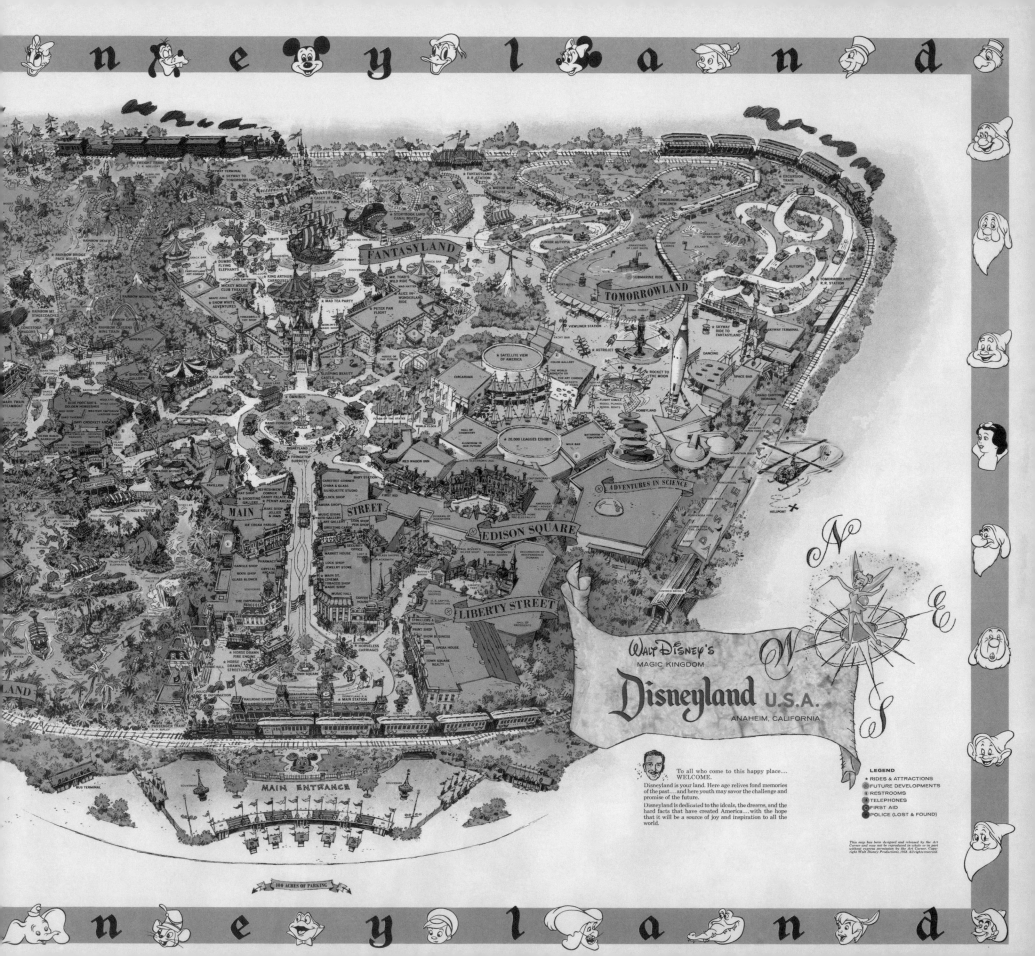

Walt Disney's

MAGIC KINGDOM

Disneyland U.S.A.

ANAHEIM, CALIFORNIA

To all who come to this happy place...
WELCOME.

Disneyland is your land. Here age relives fond memories
of the past.... and here youth may savor the challenge and
promise of the future.

Disneyland is dedicated to the ideals, the dreams, and the
hard facts that have created America...with the hope
that it will be a source of joy and inspiration to all the
world.

LEGEND

★ RIDES & ATTRACTIONS
⊙ FUTURE DEVELOPMENTS
ⓘ RESTROOMS
☎ TELEPHONES
✚ FIRST AID
● POLICE (LOST & FOUND)

Chapter 11
RECIPES OF YESTERYEAR

Granny was looking for meals that could be cooked and placed on the table.
—Tamara, Walt's Granddaughter

It's a thriller of a sundae! And note it is built in luscious *layers*—a big spoonful of strawberry sauce in bottom, then scoop of vanilla ice cream, *more* sauce, *more* ice cream, steeple of whipped cream, and berry

Sundae choo-choo sets kids agog—adults, too! Smokestack is marshmallow—see the whipped-cream smoke! Wheels are banana; cowcatcher is sugar wafers; headlight, caboose are cherries. Trio of ice creams, sauces

Topper—whipped cream, almond bits, cherry—towers high, reminiscent of a Gibson Girl pompadour. Beneath are three scoops ice cream drenched in sundae sauce. For marbling, run knife down side, lift up

It *is* the Gay '90s in every detail at the Ice Cream Parlor on Main Street. How about a cherry soda or mug of cocoa? Or indulge your sweet tooth in a colossal sundae—see at left →

Cut a good ripe banana in sled runners. Fill between with scoops of ice cream—ladle strawberry *and* marshmallow sauces over vanilla; chocolate on chocolate; crushed pineapple on strawberry. Now *flood* dish with *all four* sauces

Fresh-fruit salad plate has *drama*. Hub is sherbet (or cottage cheese) with arches of apple, peach, and whipped cream—romaine plumes

Gay '90s favorites from
Main Street, Disneyland

DO AS THEY DO in Disneyland—with an assist from the ice-cream carton—to recapture the treats of yesteryear. These happy ideas are from the famous Ice Cream Parlor, The Coffee House, and Red Wagon Inn, all located on Main Street, U.S.A.

More on page 129

The Coffee House boasts exact replicas of turn-of-the century furnishings in all their plush elegance. To go with that hospitable cup of coffee, choose hot-fudge ice-cream cake. Or strawberry shortcake (biscuit top is inverted to hold more berries!)

Photographs: de Gennaro

Nothing like a sirloin-steak sandwich for hungry folks on the go. Rest your feet, while steak broils. Meat is propped on toast to catch every drop of juice, is served with crisp French Fries, onion rings

In a hurry to ride the horsecar or play the nickelodeons? Then make your lunch the Paul Bunyan chilled meat platter—husky slices of baked ham, turkey breast, Swiss cheese, with Potato Salad

HOME

DISNEY HOME RELISH TRAY

*Anyone who wants to eat like Walt should
present a relish tray before dinner.*

Serving platter with 1-inch rim
Crushed ice
Radishes, tops and bottoms cut off
Scallions, trimmed
Pickles
Carrot sticks
Celery sticks
Turnip sticks

Place crushed ice on platter. Arrange vegetables on top.
Keep cool until ready to serve.

*There are two chili and bean recipes attributed to Walt. Make
them both for yourself and decide which you prefer. If you opt
for the 1961 version, you may need to substitute a vegetable
shortening or lard for the suet. Whatever you decide, note that
both recipes cook for at least five hours.*

CHILI AND BEANS

1958

*This version is from Walt's "Favorite Recipes" files in the
Walt Disney Archives. The exact date of origin is unknown;
however, it's marked as revised on March 25, 1958.
If you want to eat like Walt, be sure you have
crackers on hand (but not in your pockets).*

Serves 6 to 8

2 pounds dry pink beans
2 onions, sliced
2 pounds coarse ground beef
2 cloves garlic, minced
½ cup oil
1 cup chopped celery
1 teaspoon chili powder (more or less to taste)
1 teaspoon paprika
1 teaspoon dry mustard
1 large can solid pack tomatoes
Salt

Soak beans overnight in cold water, drain, add water to cover (2
inches over beans), and simmer with onions until tender (about 4
hours).

Meanwhile, prepare sauce by browning meat and minced
garlic in oil. Add remaining ingredients and simmer 1 hour.
When beans are tender, add sauce to beans and continue to
simmer for a half hour.

*These suggestions may have come from the chefs at the studio or
Disneyland; Walt wasn't a fan of highly seasoned food:*

Add a pinch of the following for a punch of flavor:

Coriander seeds
Turmeric
Chili seeds
Cumin seeds
Fennel seeds
Cloves
Cinnamon
Dry ginger
1 little yellow Mexican chili pepper

CHILI AND BEANS

1961

This recipe may be older than the official Disney version, despite being published in Kings in the Kitchen: Favorite Recipes of Famous Men *in 1961. It has more garlic and chili powder and includes chopped chili peppers. Canned kidney beans replace dried beans and tomatoes are not called for at all. You may substitute lard or vegetable shortening for the suet.*

Serves 8 to 10

½ pound suet, chopped
3 cloves garlic, minced
2 pounds ground beef
3 tablespoons chili powder
1½ teaspoons paprika
1 tablespoon salt
½ teaspoon pepper
1 teaspoon cumin seed
2 chili peppers, crushed
3 cups water
2 large cans kidney beans

Fry suet in a heavy kettle. Add garlic, meat, and seasoning. Cover and cook slowly for 4 hours, stirring occasionally. Add water and cook for 45 minutes, then add beans and cook another 15 minutes.

BROWNED ROAST BEEF HASH
(one portion)

Prime rib of beef chopped fine.
One onion chopped fine, smothered with butter and fried.
One medium sized potato chopped in very small pieces.
Mix together and add one cup of beef stock.
Put in pan in oven (350°) for one hour. Form it like
an omellette, then place in frying pan and brown.
Serve with one egg on top.

BROWNED ROAST BEEF HASH

This recipe is also from Walt's "Favorite Recipes" files in the Walt Disney Archives. The exact date is unknown. However, it may be from the sixties, as we know it was sent to the nonprofit organization Handy-Cap Horizons for a fund-raising cookbook in 1965. The instructions as presented are a head-scratcher. My trusted taste tester Maxine and I tried multiple versions. The one cup of broth and no binder are baffling; if one added enough meat (no measurement provided) to absorb all the liquid, there would be way more than one portion. And there is no mention of salt or pepper. Perhaps someone in Walt's office asked Thelma for her recipe? It's plausible she casually dictated it since she never wrote her recipes down. The answer may be lost to Disney culinary history, but there still is fun to be had with this rare recipe. Either play with it yourself or follow Disney food writer Pam Brandon and the Disney Chefs' interpretation from Chef Mickey: Treasures from the Vault & Delicious New Favorites.

Serves 4

6 tablespoons butter, divided
1½ cups finely chopped onion
2 cups (about 1 pound) finely chopped precooked prime rib
or leftover steak or roast beef
3 cups finely chopped, peeled potatoes
1 cup beef stock
Coarse salt and freshly ground pepper, to taste
4 eggs, poached or fried

Preheat oven to 350 degrees. Butter the bottom and sides of a
2-quart baking dish.

Lighty sauté onion in 4 tablespoons of butter in a large skillet
over a medium heat for 3 to 4 minutes, or until translucent and
tender.

Stir in meat, potato, and stock. Transfer ingredients into the
baking dish and bake for 1 hour. Remove from oven.

Melt the remaining 2 tablespoons of butter in a large skillet
over medium heat. Spread the hash mixture evenly in the skillet,
seasoning to taste. Cook over medium-high heat until golden
brown on the bottom, about 5 minutes. Turn the hash over with a
spatula, and cook until golden brown, about 5 minutes.

Spoon into serving plates and top with a fried or poached egg.
Serve immediately.

MORE FROM MARCY: Even though poached eggs are an option
in this updated recipe, purists will use one fried egg, just like Walt.

CLAM CHOWDER
MARCH 28, 1934
*Walt was a big fan of soups. Serve with warm bread
to mop the bowl clean, just like Walt did.*

Serves 8 to 10

6 large potatoes
6 slices of bacon, finely cut
6 onions, chopped
4 cans minced clams
2 small cans condensed milk
1 quart milk

Boil potatoes in 3 quarts of water until tender.
Peel and dice. Return to pot. In a skillet, fry bacon and onions
together.

Put in pot with potatoes.

Add clams, condensed milk, and milk. Bring soup to a
simmer. (Do not boil, as the mixture will separate.)
Ladle into warm bowls and serve.

FOU FOU STYLE GREEN BEANS

*While Walt wasn't a big fan of vegetables, this was a family
favorite. Fou Fou used only the freshest of ingredients,
so please, no canned or frozen beans.*

Serves 8

4 cups trimmed fresh green beans
Kosher salt
8 strips thick bacon, chopped
Mixed dried herbs to taste
3 tablespoons Bermuda onion, minced
Salt and pepper to taste

Drop beans in salted boiling water and cook until crisp tender,
about 5 minutes. (The fresher the green beans, the faster they will
cook.) Using a slotted spoon, transfer immediately to an ice bath.
When they are completely cooled, drain in colander and pat dry.

In a large skillet, cook bacon over medium heat until soft,
about 3 to 4 minutes. Add herbs and cook until fragrant, about
2 minutes. Mix in Bermuda onions and cook until translucent,
taking care not to burn the bacon.

Turn off the heat and stir in green beans.

Add salt and pepper to taste.

Serve immediately.

MORE FROM TAMARA: "Fou Fou would say, 'Keep that bacon
fat right there!'"

MARSHMALLOW PUDDING

MARCH 28, 1934
Dessert. Plain and simple.

Serves 4

PUDDING
2 teaspoons Knox gelatin
½ cup cold water
1 cup hot water
1 cup sugar
2 eggs, separated (save yolks for sauce)
1 lemon, juiced
Whipped cream (optional)

In a medium bowl, dissolve gelatin in cold water for 15 minutes.
Add 1 cup boiling water. Cool.

In a clean mixing bowl, whisk or beat egg whites until stiff.

In a slow and steady stream, add cooled gelatin to the beaten
egg whites. Slowly, mix in the sugar. Whisk in the lemon juice.

Set aside while you make the sauce.

SAUCE
2 cups milk
2 yolks from separated eggs
2 tablespoons sugar
1 teaspoon vanilla

Warm the milk over medium heat. (Be careful to scald, not boil,
the sauce.) Using a rubber or silicone spatula, mix in the egg yolks
and sugar. Add the vanilla.

Stir constantly for 15 minutes. Remove from heat.

Put pudding in serving bowls. Pour sauce on top and add
whipped cream, if desired.

SOFT GINGERBREAD

MARCH 28, 1934
It's not a pie, but it is a treat that Walt enjoyed.

Serves 9

1 teaspoon baking soda
¾ cup hot water
¼ cup butter, room temperature
¼ cup Crisco, room temperature
¼ cup sugar
1 egg, well beaten
1 cup molasses (Lightly coat measuring cup with
cooking spray so molasses will slip out easily)
2 cups flour, sifted
1 teaspoon ginger
1 teaspoon cinnamon

Preheat oven to 350 degrees.

Dissolve baking soda in hot water. Set aside.

Using mixer, cream butter, Crisco, and sugar for 3 minutes.

Scrape bowl then add egg, molasses, flour, ginger, and cinnamon. Blend until combined.

Add water mixture to batter. Beat until smooth, about 1 minute.

Grease and flour an 8 × 8-inch pan. Pour in batter.

Bake 20 to 30 minutes or until a toothpick inserted in the center comes out clean.

Let cool and cut into nine even pieces.

CHRIS'S COLD PIE

This recipe was found in 1974's Five Star Favorites: Recipes from Friends of Mamie and Ike *under the name Mrs. John Truyens. (Truyens was Lillian's second husband's last name.)*

Serves 8

4 eggs, separated
½ cup lemon juice
½ cup water
1 tablespoon unflavored gelatin
1 cup sugar
¼ teaspoon salt
1 tablespoon grated lemon rind
1 graham cracker crust
(premade, boxed mix, or from scratch)
Nutmeg

In a small bowl, beat egg yolks with lemon juice and water until just combined.

Mix gelatin, half the sugar, and the salt in the top of a double boiler. Pour in egg-yolk mixture, blending well.

Cook, stirring constantly, over boiling water (water should not touch top section of double boiler) until gelatin dissolves and mixture thickens.

Remove top from boiling water. Stir in lemon rind.

Let set 20 minutes in a bowl filled with ice cubes, stirring occasionally.

Remove from ice when mixture thickens enough to mound when dropped from a spoon.

Meanwhile, beat egg whites (at room temperature) in a large bowl until soft peaks form when beater is raised.

Gradually add remaining sugar, 2 tablespoons at a time, beating well after each addition.

Continue beating until stiff peaks form when batter is raised.

Gently fold gelatin mixture into egg whites until just combined.

Turn filling into piecrust. Dust top with nutmeg and chill several hours. (If desired, omit nutmeg and serve topped with whipped cream.)

CHINESE CANDY COOKIES
When I made these for Walt's granddaughter Jenny, she took one look at them and exclaimed, "You made my grandfather's cookies!"

Makes about 2 dozen cookies

12-ounce package butterscotch chips
2 cups chow mein noodles
1 cup roasted peanuts

It's easy to burn butterscotch. I prefer to melt carefully over very low heat. If you use a double boiler, be sure no water splashes into pot (that will turn the butterscotch into a lumpy paste).

Remove from heat. Pour over noodles and peanuts. Mix well.
Using a teaspoon, drop mixture onto waxed paper. Let cool.

MORE FROM JENNY: "After Grandpa died, Fou Fou was with us a lot longer, [and] she always had these in the cookie jar with the wax paper around them."

SCOTCH MIST
If you want to drink like Walt, use Black & White or Canadian Club. And if you're the sentimental type, listen to "Feed the Birds" while sipping your cocktail.

Serves 1

Crushed ice
2–3 ounces of Scotch
Twist of lemon peel or orange slice
Long silver or plastic spoon (optional)

Pack crushed ice into a glass. Pour Scotch over ice.
Garnish with lemon or orange.

STUDIO

MACARONI MICKEY MOUSSE

Before pasta, there was macaroni, the generic name for all dried noodles. Without a time machine, it's hard to know exactly what type of "macaroni" Walt's cook used. "Broken into 2-inch pieces" indicates it was likely spaghetti, but feel free to substitute elbow macaroni or other short tubular pasta.

Serves 6

1 cup uncooked macaroni broken into 2-inch pieces
1½ cups milk
1 cup bread crumbs
¼ cup butter (one half stick), melted
1 pimiento, aka cherry pepper, minced, or 1 teaspoon bottled minced pimientos
1 tablespoon chopped parsley
1 tablespoon chopped onion
1½ cups grated cheese
1 teaspoon salt
⅛ teaspoon pepper
Dash paprika
3 eggs, beaten

Preheat oven to 325 degrees.
Cook the macaroni in salted water, drain, cover with cold water, and drain again. Set aside.
  Scald the milk in the pasta pot.

Put bread crumbs in a large bowl. Pour scalded milk over bread crumbs. Mix well.

Add melted butter, pimiento, parsley, onion, grated cheese, salt, pepper, and paprika.

Fold in beaten eggs.

Grease a loaf pan (shallow casseroles make for a drier result).

Place macaroni on bottom of pan and pour cheese mixture over it.

Bake 50 minutes or until firm.

Let cool 10 minutes, then turn over on a platter and serve.

MORE FROM WALT: Substitute the parsley for two teaspoons of finely chopped celery and add two strips of finely chopped cooked bacon.

MORE FROM MARCY: When you see the paltry amount of pasta, you may be concerned the dish wouldn't be enough for Mickey and Minnie, much less six hungry guests. Fear not; with the generous cheese sauce, it's plenty.

TEA LOUNGE TEA CAKES

These square cupcakes have achieved mythical status in southern California for nearly a century. Fans flock to Martino's Bakery and buy them by the dozens. In 1994 the new owners inherited the secret recipe but they are keeping it, well, secret. Enter baker Johanna Lasseter-Curtis (my pal and John Lasseter's twin sister). She tasted and tested— with a little culinary CSI—until she could come close to the tea cakes of Walt's day.

Makes 12
(Or a baker's dozen, a nod to Walt's favorite number: 13)

Fill *square* cupcake pans with white 2- x 1⅜-inch round cupcake liners. Tempting as the matching square liners are, do not use them; they're too big. If you use the smaller traditional supermarket liners, yield will increase. Do not grease or spray liners.

BATTER
1½ cup all purpose flour
1 teaspoon baking powder
¼ teaspoon salt
1 cup vegetable oil
2 tablespoons (1 ounce) butter or margarine at room temperature
1 cup golden brown sugar, packed
1 cup granulated white sugar
⅔ cup buttermilk at room temperature
1 teaspoon vanilla
⅛ teaspoon or 2 to 3 drops lemon extract
2 large eggs

Preheat oven to 350 degrees.

Sift dry ingredients together in separate bowl. Set aside.

Using an electric mixer, cream oil, butter or margarine, brown and white sugar for 1 minute on medium-high speed; scrape bowl, mix 1 more minute.

Add buttermilk, vanilla, lemon extract, and eggs. Mix on low to combine.

Add dry ingredients. Mix on medium-high for 1 minute, scrape bowl, mix 1 minute more.

Using an ice cream scoop or ⅓ measuring cup, fill cupcake liners ¾ full of batter.

Bake 24 to 28 minutes until the tea cakes are golden brown with a slight dome and spring back from touch, or a toothpick inserted in the center comes out clean.

Let tea cakes rest 5 minutes in pan, then remove immediately.

Cool an additional 15 minutes. Meanwhile, make the glaze.

GLAZE
2 cups powdered sugar
3 tablespoons (1.5 ounces) butter or margarine
4 tablespoons water
2 tablespoons golden brown sugar, packed
1 teaspoon vanilla
1-2 drops yellow food coloring
Wax or parchment paper

Sift powdered sugar. Set aside.

Melt butter or margarine in medium saucepan.

Add water and brown sugar, cooking until sugar dissolves.

Do not boil. Remove from heat.

Mix in vanilla and food coloring.

Immediately whisk in powdered sugar until smooth.

If glaze is too thick, you can gently reheat. If glaze is too thin, add a little more powdered sugar.

Dip the tops of the cooled teacakes into warm glaze and place on wax or parchment paper to harden, about 5 minutes.

MORE FROM MARCY: Johanna and I made a conscious decision to use the mid-century ingredients of Walt's era, thus the options of margarine and food coloring. Square cupcake pans are a must! I prefer Wilton. You'll find them easily online.

MAIN STREET, U.S.A.

OSCAR'S POTATOES
Carnation Café

Oscar is a legend. He was the most requested media interview for Disneyland's fiftieth anniversary and celebrated his sixtieth anniversary as a Disneyland employee in December 2016.

Serves 6 to 8

2 pounds red potatoes, sliced ¼ inch or thicker
1 medium white onion, julienned
6 tablespoons butter
Salt and pepper to taste

Preheat oven to 400 degrees.

Sauté onions in 2 tablespoons of butter until softened. Set aside.

In a 12-inch skillet (don't crowd the potatoes), sauté potatoes with the remainder of the butter. Keep cooking until the potatoes are browned and add the onions. Season with salt and pepper.

Transfer potato mixture to a new pan; 8 x 10 inches works well. Then cover with parchment paper and foil. Poke holes in foil for ventilation.

Bake for 40 minutes to 1 hour.

Taste and correct for salt and pepper as needed.

MORE FROM OSCAR: "You have to stay with the potatoes. You can't walk away. They need to be basted with butter every five minutes."

WOODEN BARREL DILL PICKLES

Swift Market House

Dill pickles don't grow on bushes, so here's a foolproof way to make your own. Sliced thin, they're great as a garnish.

For 10 to 12 pickles, depending on their size

1-gallon jar
3 tablespoons pickling spice
3 cloves garlic
10–12 cucumbers (or enough to fill your jar)
4 heaping teaspoons kosher salt
3 cloves garlic
1 package fresh dill
Water to cover

Pour boiling water in jar to clean. Pour out. Drop pickling spices and garlic in bottom of jar. Place cucumbers in jar just up to the neck. Top with salt and dill. Add water and cover securely. Shake up and down and let stand for 3 to 4 days before serving.

SPRINGTIME PEAS

Red Wagon Inn

These sweet peas are popular with kids.

Serves 4

2 pounds fresh peas, shelled
3–6 lettuce leaves
⅓ cup sliced green onions
1 teaspoon sugar
½ teaspoon salt
Dash pepper
Dash thyme

3 tablespoons butter or margarine, cut into small cubes

Cover bottom of skillet with lettuce. Top with peas and onions. Sprinkle seasonings on top. Add butter.

Cover tightly and cook over low heat 10 to 15 minutes or until peas are done.

Remove peas and serve immediately.

MORE FROM MARCY: You may replace fresh peas with frozen (not defrosted) peas. Cook for 5 minutes.

POTATO SALAD

Red Wagon Inn

This was a staple of the restaurant, served with sandwiches and the Paul Bunyan Cold Meat Platter.

Serves 8

4 cups peeled and cubed potatoes
(about 6 potatoes; recommend boiling in skins)
3 hard-cooked eggs, chopped
1 cup chopped celery
1½ teaspoons salt
¼ teaspoon paprika
¼ cup bottled French dressing
Mayonnaise

Combine cubed potatoes, chopped eggs, celery, salt, and paprika. Add French dressing. Chill 4 to 6 hours. Before serving, add just enough mayonnaise to moisten salad.

Serve with a salad scoop.

BEETS PIQUANT

Red Wagon Inn

Piquant means interesting and exciting. It also means tart and agreeably pungent. These mid-century sweet-and-sour beets are all these things. Serve warm or cold.

Serves 4

6–7 medium beets
2 tablespoons butter or margarine
2 tablespoons lemon juice (fresh, frozen, or canned)
1 tablespoon sugar
½ teaspoon salt
2 tablespoons chopped parsley

Pare fresh beets. With sharp knife, cut in thin strips.

Melt butter in skillet. Add beets; sprinkle with lemon juice, sugar, and salt.

Cook, covered, over low heat 15 to 20 minutes or until tender. Sprinkle with parsley.

MORE FROM MARCY: Rather than peel and cut the raw beet as suggested in this 1957 recipe, a simpler method is to parboil the beets, drain, run under cool water, and use a paper towel to remove the skins. Julienne and prepare as above, reducing cooking time to 10 to 12 minutes.

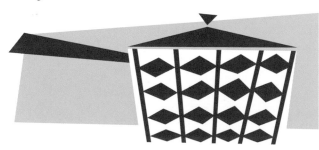

SANTA FE EXPRESS SUNDAE

Maxwell House Coffee House

"It's a thriller of a sundae!" A tribute to Walt's Santa Fe and Disneyland railroad.

Strawberry sauce (homemade or store-bought)
Vanilla ice cream
Strawberry ice cream
Chocolate ice cream
Hot fudge sauce (recipe follows)
Marshmallows
Whipped cream
Banana, cut into 1-inch pieces
Sugar wafers
Maraschino cherries

Place strawberry sauce on the bottom of a shallow banana split bowl.

Add 1 scoop each of vanilla, strawberry, and chocolate ice cream.

Top with hot fudge sauce.

Make a smokestack with stacked marshmallows.

Use whipped cream for the smoke coming out of the stack.

Banana slices make the wheels on each side.

Use sugar wafers to form a cowcatcher. (Create an inverted V at the front.)

Place a cherry in front for headlight and another in the back for the caboose.

MORE FROM MARCY: There is a photograph of the original sundae on page 149 that may be helpful with the assembly.

HOT FUDGE SAUCE
Makes about 1 cup

2 ounces unsweetened chocolate
⅓ cup water
½ cup sugar
Dash salt
3 tablespoons butter
¼ teaspoon vanilla

Combine chocolate and water. Stir over low heat until blended.
Add sugar and salt. Cook slowly, stirring constantly,
until sugar dissolves and mixture thickens slightly.
Add butter and vanilla. Serve warm.

APPLE PIE
Plaza Inn
This pie is from Walt's favorite restaurant at Disneyland.

Serves 8–10

PASTRY
2 cups flour
½ teaspoon salt
6 tablespoons solid vegetable shortening
2 tablespoons butter, chilled
½ cup (or as needed) orange juice, chilled

Mix flour and salt in a bowl. Add shortening and butter. With a
pastry blender or fork, cut butter and shortening into flour until
crumbly. Gradually add orange juice until dough holds together.
Knead dough very lightly and form into two balls. Wrap in plastic
wrap and refrigerate while preparing filling.

FILLING
3 pounds baking apples
1 lemon, juiced
¾ cup sugar
1 teaspoon cinnamon
⅛ teaspoon salt
4 tablespoons butter

Peel and core apples. Cut into ½-inch slices and place in a large
bowl. Sprinkle with lemon juice and mix with sugar, cinnamon,
and salt. Let mixture sit 10 minutes at room temperature.
Preheat oven to 425 degrees.
On a floured board, roll out one ball of pastry and fit into the
bottom of a 9-inch pie plate. Add filling and dot top with chilled
butter. Roll out remaining pastry and cover apples, sealing edges
carefully. Prick the top of the pie with the point of a paring knife
to allow steam to escape.
Bake for 10 minutes. Reduce heat to 350 degrees and continue
baking for at least an additional 40 to 50 minutes. Remove pie and
allow to cool before serving.

PEANUT BRITTLE
Candy Palace
*Disneyland's iconic candymaker, Lee Hight, offers this
advice: "Pay strict attention to recipes, and always measure
exactly. Candy making can't be 'a pinch of this and a pinch
of that' type of cooking. And temperatures are very important
—be exact and use a thermometer when it's called for,
or you'll change the character of your candy. Sometimes
it just takes experience; your first batch may not be perfect,
but you've got to try again. It will get better each time."*

Makes about 1½ pounds of candy

1½ cups sugar
½ cup corn syrup (white Karo)
½ cup water
1 cup raw Spanish peanuts (unsalted)
2 tablespoons margarine or butter
1 teaspoon vanilla
½ teaspoon salt
½ teaspoon baking soda (or 1 teaspoon for fluffier texture)

In a 2-quart saucepan, combine sugar, corn syrup, and water. Place candy on high heat and begin cooking. Bring candy to a boil, then wash down inside of pan with water and a pastry brush. This is to prevent candy from sugaring off. Use a candy thermometer and cook candy until it reaches 240 degrees, and then add raw Spanish peanuts and turn heat to medium.

Continue cooking to 260 degrees and add margarine or butter. At this point, stir batch with a wooden spoon until candy is cooked to 294 degrees. Turn off heat and add vanilla; mix in well. Add salt and soda, and mix in well.

Pour completed candy out on a greased cookie sheet pan. (Modern-day Silpat, or parchment, lightly greased or sprayed, works very well.)

Spread out and allow to cool slightly. Turn over and stretch to desired thinness. Cool completely, then break up.

ADVENTURELAND

PINEAPPLE POLYNESIAN RIBS
Tahitian Terrace
The vintage name for this dish is Ko'aia Haia Kahiki.

Serves 4

2 cups tomato ketchup
¼ cup soy sauce
¼ cup pineapple juice
¼ cup crushed pineapple (fresh or canned)
¼ cup fresh orange juice
1 teaspoon grated orange rind
½ cup brown sugar
1 tablespoon wine vinegar
3 whole cloves
4 pounds pork spareribs or baby back ribs

Combine all ingredients (except ribs) and blend well. Allow mixture to stand in refrigerator overnight.

Strain before using.

Preheat oven to 275 degrees.

Place ribs on a rack in roasting pan or sheet pan.

Bake, basting with sauce often, for 2 to 3 hours, or until meat separates easily from the bone.

MORE FROM MARCY: There is quite a bit of salt in the ketchup and soy sauce—you may not need any salt or rub on the ribs. The Disneyland recipe calls for the ribs to be precut before cooking, but that can dry them out. So, I recommend roasting the racks intact and slicing just before serving. The leftover sauce freezes nicely.

CHOW YUK STIR FRY

Tahitian Terrace
Chow Yuk is the name of an authentic
Chinese dish featuring sautéed vegetables and meat.

Serves 4

2 tablespoons vegetable oil
6 ounces turkey breast meat, sliced
(or chicken, pork, beef, or veal)
1 teaspoon salt
½ cup sliced onion
1½ cups thinly sliced celery
½ cup sliced fresh mushrooms
¼ cup sliced bamboo shoots
¼ cup sliced water chestnuts
1 cup chicken broth
¼ cup Chinese pea pods, cut in half
1 tablespoon cornstarch
2 tablespoons water
Hot cooked rice or noodles

Heat oil in large skillet or wok. Add turkey and salt and stir-fry until turkey is lightly browned. Add onion, celery, mushrooms, bamboo shoots, and water chestnuts.

Stir-fry until tender but still a little crispy. Add broth and pea-pods and simmer 2 to 3 minutes.

Mix cornstarch with water and add to skillet. Bring mixture to a full boil, stirring constantly, for 1 minute. Remove from heat.

Serve over rice or noodles.

MAHIMAHI

Tahitian Terrace
Please don't wince at the yellow food coloring.
You may omit it, but if you want to eat like Walt, don't.

Serves 6

SAUCE
2 cups pineapple juice
1 cup sugar
2½ tablespoons cornstarch
¾ cup apple cider vinegar
½ cup tomato ketchup
½ cup pineapple tidbits

In a small saucepan, combine pineapple juice, sugar, and cornstarch. Add remaining ingredients. Stir until mixture comes to a boil and is thickened. Set over low heat to keep warm while you fry the fish.

MAHIMAHI
1 cup cold water
1 egg
1 teaspoon salt
2 teaspoons vegetable oil
1 cup flour
⅛ teaspoon yellow food coloring
6 boneless mahimahi fillets (or other firm whitefish)
Oil for frying

In a mixing bowl, combine water, egg, salt, and vegetable oil.

Beat slowly to blend. Gradually add flour, beating to form a smooth batter. Add food coloring if desired.

Dip fish fillets into batter and fry in hot oil (350 degrees) until golden brown (5 to 6 minutes).

Remove and drain on absorbent towels.

Serve with sauce.

HAWAIIAN GINGER DRESSING
Tahitian Terrace

*A mixture of greens and chopped romaine lettuce
makes a lovely base for this salad dressing.*

Makes 1½ cups dressing

7 tablespoons red wine vinegar
5 tablespoons vegetable oil
3 tablespoons peeled and chopped ginger (fresh)
1 tablespoon garlic salt
8 tablespoons crushed pineapple
3 tablespoons sugar

In a blender, combine vinegar, oil, and fresh ginger. Blend well on high speed for 15 seconds. Add salt, pineapple, and sugar. Blend another 15 seconds.

Refrigerate until ready to use.

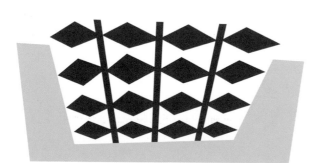

TAHITIAN TERRACE PUNCH
Tahitian Terrace

*"A blend of the exotic fresh juices of the Islands.
Served in a tall frosted glass with a flower memento."*

Makes 2½ quarts

¾ cup pineapple juice
3 tablespoons grenadine
3 tablespoons lemon juice
11½-ounce can Welch's Grape Juice concentrate
(white or Concord)
½ cup sugar
3 tablespoons Tang Orange Powdered Drink
5 cups water

Combine all the ingredients until well mixed. Serve over ice.

MORE FROM MARCY: I am all for purists. However, I find the punch is more refreshing without the added sugar. For the adult version, add a splash or two—or more—of rum.

FRONTIERLAND

TA-CUP

Casa De Fritos

Try as I might, I could not find a recipe for the Ta-cup, so I created my own. Every order at Casa de Fritos was served with a bag of Fritos. If you want to honor the Frito Kid, put a small bag of the corn chips on the plate, too.

Serves 8

Eight 5½- to 6-inch corn tortillas
1 pound hamburger
1 package taco seasoning (or season to taste)
Red taco sauce
1½ cups shredded iceberg or romaine lettuce
8 heaping tablespoons of cheese (or more to taste)
Vegetable oil for frying, or cooking spray if baking
Black olives

Ready-made tortilla bowls are sold in the market, but that eliminates the fun of re-creating the original. There are also basket molds that make tortilla shells. However, I found most require 8-inch tortillas; flour-based ones come that large, but not those made of corn (and we are in Frito-Lay land here). Plus, they use a lot of cooking oil. The mini 4½-inch tortilla baking molds work very well and are a healthy alternative. Nothing, however, beats freshly fried, and those will be closer to the original.

FRIED TORTILLA BOWLS

Preheat oven to 325 degrees.

Fill a 2-quart saucepan two-thirds full with oil. Heat until a piece of tortilla dropped into it "oil dances," about 375 degrees.

Place one tortilla on a spider or slotted spoon. Using silicone tongs, press on the center of the tortilla and submerge in oil. Keep the tongs in place as this will shape the tortilla bowl.

Remove, drain on a paper towel, and repeat with remaining tortillas. Be careful to monitor heat of oil.

Wrap the tortilla bowls loosely in foil and place in oven to keep warm.

BAKED TORTILLA BOWLS

Preheat oven to 350 degrees.

Microwave tortillas 15 seconds.

Spray molds with cooking spray and put warm tortillas inside the molds.

Place on a baking sheet and bake 5 to 8 minutes or until golden brown.

Reduce heat to 325. Wrap tortilla bowls loosely in foil and place in oven to keep warm. (If you have four molds, bake a second batch and keep warm with others.)

TA-CUPS

Prepare ground beef with seasonings.

Fill each Ta-cup with equal parts ground beef and shredded lettuce. Add red sauce and top with cheese. Garnish with black olive.

Serve immediately.

MORE FROM DOOLIN: "You're supposed to eat a taco with your hands. Now it can be eaten like an open sandwich."

SILVER BANJO BARBECUE SAUCE

Don Defore's Silver Banjo
Don's sons, Dave and Ron, grew up at Disneyland.
They graciously shared their family recipe.

Makes 3 quarts

6 cups (48 ounces) Hunt's tomato sauce
1½ cups Heinz chili sauce (one 12-ounce bottle)
1 cup water (if needed, add more water to taste)
¾ cup Pompeian red wine vinegar
¼ cup Lea & Perrins Worcestershire sauce
¼ cup Kikkoman soy sauce
¾ cup (unsulfured) molasses, Grandma's or Blackstrap molasses
2¼ cups sugar (add more or less to taste)
4 teaspoons Colman's mustard powder
4 teaspoons McCormick celery seed (not celery salt)
1 teaspoon black pepper
½ teaspoon cinnamon
½ teaspoon dry garlic powder
½ teaspoon dry onion powder
1 teaspoon Colgin liquid hickory smoke
(add more to taste, but be careful)

Combine all ingredients and simmer 2 to 3 hours, the longer the better. Barbecue sauce is best the next day.

FANTASYLAND

TUNABURGERS

Chicken of the Sea Pirate Ship and Restaurant
While there are several similar recipes, this is the authentic tuna-burger recipe as written in a Chicken of the Sea recipe pamphlet in 1956. Purists will want to use the same mermaid brand that sponsored the restaurant and attraction for fourteen years.

Serves 4

One 6½-ounce can Chicken of the Sea brand tuna
1 tablespoon chopped onion
¼ cup chopped celery
1 teaspoon lemon juice
¼ cup mayonnaise
2 tablespoons ketchup
Sweet pickle slices
4 whole hamburger buns sliced in 3 horizontal sections

Preheat oven to 375 degrees.

Mix tuna with onion, celery, lemon juice, and half of the mayonnaise. Make dressing by blending remaining mayonnaise with ketchup.

Spread dressing on bottom slices. Cover with pickles. Spread tuna mixture on middle slices. Add top bun to create a double-decker sandwich. Wrap in foil.

Bake 15 minutes and serve hot.

MORE FROM MARCY: For smoother sailing, use standard precut sesame hamburger buns, as suggested on the restaurant's place mat for home cooks.

NEW ORLEANS SQUARE

MONTE CRISTO

Blue Bayou Restaurant
Get out the twinkle lights and set
"Yo Ho (A Pirate's Life for Me)" on repeat.

Serves 4

1 egg
1¾ cups plus 2 tablespoons water
1¾ cups all-purpose flour
¼ teaspoon salt
1 teaspoon baking powder
8 slices egg bread (challah works well), sliced ½-inch thick
8 thin slices ham
8 thin slices turkey
8 thin slices Swiss cheese
3 cups canola oil
Powdered sugar
Blackberry preserves, optional
Raspberry jelly, optional

Line a cookie sheet with paper towels; set aside.

Whisk the egg and water together in a mixing bowl. Add flour, salt, and baking powder and whisk thoroughly for 2 to 3 minutes, or until smooth, scraping the side of the bowl.

On one slice of bread, arrange 2 slices of ham, turkey, and cheese, covering the bread evenly. Place another slice of bread on top and slice each sandwich in half diagonally.

Heat oil between 365 degrees and 375 degrees in a 10-inch pan. Do not let the oil reach a higher temperature than this; if the oil starts to smoke, turn the heat down. Dip half of the sandwich into the batter, allowing excess to drain, and very carefully place in oil.

Cook 3 minutes on each side, or until golden brown. Repeat with the other sandwich half. Place the cooked sandwich on the prepared cookie sheet in a warm oven until ready to serve. Repeat with the other three sandwiches. Cook one at a time, and allow the oil to reach the desired temperature between each.

Sprinkle with powdered sugar and serve with the blackberry preserves or raspberry jelly on the side.

INDIAN'S COCONUT SAUCE

Indian's original recipes, typewritten on index cards (with many including MSG), are in the Walt Disney Archives. Naturally, they were written in restaurant quantities; however, I interpreted his coconut sauce, which was more like gravy, for the home cook. It goes very well with one of Walt's favorites—roast chicken.

Yields about 2 cups

2 slices bacon cut into small pieces
½ cup minced onion
2 tablespoons coconut oil
2 tablespoons flour
1 cup chicken or turkey broth
½ cup unsweetened coconut milk
1 teaspoon garlic powder
¼ teaspoon ground white pepper
1 teaspoon paprika
¼ cup dry sherry

In a 10-inch skillet, fry bacon pieces. When they're halfway cooked, about 3 to 4 minutes, mix in the chopped onions.

When onions are lightly browned, add coconut oil. Reduce heat. After oil has been absorbed, whisk in flour.

Pour in the broth slowly, scraping the brown bits as you stir.

Add the coconut milk, garlic powder, white pepper, paprika, and dry sherry. Stir to blend.

Simmer additional 10 minutes or so on low heat to thicken sauce. Salt to taste.

MORE FROM INDIAN: If you want more coconut flavor, use imitation coconut extract.

MORE FROM MARCY: Or you can use lightly toasted, unsweetened shredded coconut.

CHICKEN GUMBO
Creole Café
Enjoy Disneyland's New Orleans Gumbo
with Louisiana rice.

Serves 4

CAJUN SPICE
2 tablespoons paprika
1 tablespoon seasoning salt
2 teaspoons granulated garlic
1½ teaspoons onion powder
1½ teaspoons freshly ground black pepper
1½ teaspoons sugar
1 teaspoon cayenne
½ teaspoon freshly ground white pepper
½ teaspoon dried thyme
½ teaspoon dried oregano

Combine all ingredients in a medium bowl and set aside.

Leftover spice can be stored in an airtight container for up to 1 week.

CHICKEN GUMBO
½ cup unsalted butter
1 pound skinless boneless chicken thighs, diced
½ cup diced Tasso ham
½ cup diced andouille sausage
3 tablespoons chopped garlic
½ cup all-purpose flour
3 tablespoons Cajun spice
4 cups chicken stock
½ cup sliced okra
¼ cup diced tomatoes
¼ cup chopped green onions, for garnish

Melt butter in a Dutch oven over medium-high heat. Add chicken, Tasso ham, and andouille sausage and cook until golden brown, about 5 minutes.

Add garlic, stirring to combine. Cook until fragrant, about 1 minute.

Remove meat from pot with a slotted spoon, reserving fat in a pot. Place meat on a large plate and set aside.

Add flour to fat in the pot, whisking to combine. Cook until mixture turns golden, about 10 to 15 minutes.

Stir in Cajun spice.

Return meat to pot, stirring well to combine. Slowly add stock, whisking vigorously after each addition until mixture is smooth. Add okra and tomatoes. Simmer, stirring frequently, until okra is tender, about 10 to 15 minutes.

CAJUN RICE

1 tablespoon olive oil
1 tablespoon diced white onion
1 tablespoon diced red bell pepper
1 cup medium-grain white rice
1¾ cups vegetable stock
1 tablespoon Cajun spice

Heat oil in a large saucepan over medium heat. Add onion and bell pepper; sauté 3 minutes, or until translucent.

Add rice, stirring to coat in oil. Toast rice, stirring frequently, 3 to 4 minutes.

Add vegetable stock, stir, then add Cajun spice, stirring well.

Cover pan and bring to a boil; reduce heat to low. Cook 15 to 20 minutes, or until liquid is completely absorbed.

Fluff with a fork.

Ladle gumbo into bowls and top with a large spoonful of rice. Garnish with chopped green onions.

MINT JULEP

Mint Julep Bar near Frontierland Railroad Station
This iconic Disneyland beverage was
also sold on the Mark Twain.

Makes 2 quarts

2 cups granulated sugar
6 cups water
1¼ ounces pure lime juice concentrate
8½ ounces lemonade concentrate
2¼ ounces crème de menthe syrup (non-alcoholic)

Combine sugar and water in a medium-sized saucepan. Stir until sugar is dissolved. Stir in lime juice and lemonade concentrate. Add crème de menthe syrup and mix well.

Over medium-high heat, bring to 185 degrees F. Do not boil. Remove from heat and refrigerate until well chilled.

To make juleps, use 1 part syrup to 5 parts chilled water.

For the adult version, substitute parts bourbon for parts water to taste.

MORE FROM MARCY: Tony Baxter misses the original carbonated mint juleps served from 1966 until the mid-1980s. If you want to drink them like the former Carnation scooper and Imagineer behind Indiana Jones Adventure, mix 1 part syrup to 5 parts soda water. The signature garnish is a must: a maraschino cherry, a twist of lime, and a sprig of mint.

RECIPE INDEX

Tom Fitzgerald

AFTERWORD

Growing up on the East Coast in the 1960s, the idea of visiting Disneyland felt like an impossible dream. Fortunately for me, Walt Disney brought a little bit of Disneyland to New York, setting up four attractions at the 1964–65 World's Fair. My family visited the fair several times, and those Disney shows blew me away. I loved General Electric's Progressland with its Carousel of Progress show (my favorite); I also spent the silver dollar my grandparents gave me on a ticket to ride "it's a small world," pretended to drive the Mustang convertible in Ford's Magic Skyway past the dinosaurs, and thought history was pretty cool—for the first time—when I saw Great Moments with Mr. Lincoln at the State of Illinois pavilion.

There's no question that the Disney shows at the fair changed my life. I knew then and there I wanted to be a part of making that magic, and that I absolutely had to get to Disneyland . . . somehow! I'm a firm believer that if you can dream it you can do it, and in 1969, my family traveled all the way to California for a dream vacation.

Since this is a book about food, I should probably say that *food* (or lack of it) almost kept me from going to Disneyland. The morning of my first visit I was so excited about finally seeing the Magic Kingdom that I refused to eat breakfast. My mom's response? "No breakfast, no Disneyland." I ate breakfast.

Once inside the gates of Disneyland, my appetite magically returned. I can still recall the different meals—food experiences—during that first visit: a Chicken of the Sea Tunaburger at the Pirate Ship and Restaurant in Fantasyland, dinner at the magical and exotic Blue Bayou Restaurant in New Orleans Square, ice cream from the Carnation Ice Cream Parlor, and treats from the Candy Palace on Main Street (my mom had a sweet tooth). Every experience was part of the story and show. Even as a kid, it all resonated.

Today when visiting Disney parks around the world, food is always part of my game plan. I have to have a Dole Whip at The Enchanted Tiki Room and a drink at Trader Sam's at the Disneyland Resort; Tonga Toast at the Polynesian Village Resort at Walt Disney World; make an annual visit to Epcot's International Food & Wine Festival; have drinks at Carthay Circle at Disney California Adventure; a Gyoza Dog at Tokyo DisneySea; dinner at Palo on the Disney cruise ships. My list goes on and on.

Dining has always been an integral part of the storytelling experience in our parks. As we look to the future, our Imagineering teams are exploring new ways to immerse you deeper into our stories, adventures, and worlds through unique and varied food and beverage experiences.

People often ask, "What's in store for the future of our parks?" As Imagineers, we have a pretty good idea of the answer, because the things we are working on today you may not see for several years in our parks (or at sea).

While I can't tell you the specifics of what we're working on, I promise you'll be amazed by the innovative and entertaining dining ideas on the drawing boards. There really is a great big beautiful tomorrow. It's just a dream away . . . and it's delicious (particularly in the culinary arena)!

—TOM FITZGERALD
PORTFOLIO CREATIVE EXECUTIVE
WALT DISNEY IMAGINEERING

BIBLIOGRAPHY

Arellano, Gustavo. *Taco USA: How Mexican Food Conquered America*. Boca Raton, FL, Scribner Book Company, 2012.

Auxiliary, Eisenhower Medical Center. *Five-Star Favorites: Recipes from Friends of Mamie and Ike*. New York: Golden Press, 1974.

Booth, Gertrude. *KINGS IN THE KITCHEN: Favorite Recipes of Famous Men*. New York, New York: A. S. Barnes and Company, 1961.

Brandon, Pam and Disney Chefs. *Chef Mickey: Treasures from the Vault & Delicious New Favorites*. New York: Disney Editions, 2010.

Cline, Rebecca. "Perspiration and Pancakes." *Disney Magazine* Spring 2004.

Cline, Rebecca and Paul Anderson. "Interview with Richard Frank Jr." 2009.

Cline, Rebecca and Rob Klein. "The Blue Bayou, An 'E-Ticket' Adventure in Dining."

Disney. "Access." Accessed September 8, 2016. https://d23.com/tiki-room-50th-anniversary-archives/.

Disney, Lillian. (April 19, 1973). Bob Thomas Interview.

Disney, Walt. *Walt Disney: Conversations*. Edited by Kathy Merlock Jackson. Jackson, MS: University Press of Mississippi, 2005.

Eddy, Don. "The Amazing Secret of Walt Disney." *American Magazine* 1955: 28–29, 100–115.

Fritz. "Frito Kid and Deeee-Licious Fritos!—Imagineering Disney—" October 13, 2013. Accessed December 11, 2015. http://www.imagineeringdisney.com/blog/2010/6/26/frito-kid-and-deeee-licious-fritos.html.

"Gay '90s Favorites from Main Street, Disneyland." *Better Homes and Gardens* May 1957: 96–129.

Ghez, Didier. *Walt's People—Volume 8: Talking Disney with the Artists Who Knew Him*. Bloomington, IN: Xlibris LLC, 2009.

Gordon, Bruce, David Mumford, Roger Le Roque, and Nick Farago. *Disneyland the Nickel Tour: A Postcard Journey Through 40 Years of the Happiest Place on Earth*. Santa Clara, CA: Camphor Tree Publishers, 1995.

Hall, Joyce C and Curtiss Anderson. *When You Care Enough*. Kansas City, MO: Hallmark, 1979.

Higgins, Chris. "What Disneyland Looked Like in 1957." 1955. Accessed August 27, 2016. http://mentalfloss.com/article/29929/what-disneyland-looked-1957.

Pierce, Todd James. http://www.disneyhistoryinstitute.com/2014/03/the-penthouse-club-at-disney-studio.html

Imagineers, the Imagineers, and Alex Wright. *The Imagineering Field Guide to Disneyland: An Imagineer's-Eye Tour*. New York: Disney Editions, 2008.

Kurtti, Jeff. "The Wonderful World of WALT: Walt Disney, Educator | Disney Insider." October 8, 2012. Accessed August 1, 2016. https://ohmy.disney.com/insider/2012/10/08/the-wonderful-world-of-walt-walt-disney-educator/.

Lane, Anthony, Andrew Marantz, Shannon Reed, Benjamin Schwartz, Om Malik, Sarah Hutto, Mark Gimein, Nick Paumgarten, and Dana Goodyear. "Anthony Lane." February 13, 2015, Accessed August 26, 2016. http://www.newyorker.com/magazine/2006/12/11/wonderful-world.

"Macaroni Mickey Mousse." *Better Homes and Gardens* February 1934: 42.

macmouse4. "House of the Future—Part 1." *YouTube*. June 9, 2007. Posted August 27, 2016. https://www.youtube.com/watch?v=DoCCO3GKqWY.

MousePlanet and Jim Korkis. "Eating Like Walt Disney." August 31, 2011. Accessed May 8, 2016. https://www.mouseplanet.com/9723/Eating_Like_Walt_Disney.

MousePlanet and Wade Sampson. "The Story of the Red Wagon Inn." July 4, 2007. Accessed November 2, 2015. http://mouseplanet.com/8202/The_Story_of_the_Red_Wagon_Inn.

Noriyuki, Duane. "Thelma Howards's Legacy of Hope." *Los Angeles Times*, October 24, 1994.

Nugent, Frank. "That Million-Dollar Mouse." *The New York Times Magazine* 1947.

O'Brien, Tim. *Tony Baxter: First of the Second Generation of Walt Disney Imagineers*. United States: Casa Flamingo Literary Arts, 2015.

"On Safari." *Vacationland* 1962: 2–5.

Peri, Don. *Working with Disney: Interviews with Animators, Producers, and Artists*. Jackson: University Press of Mississippi, 2011.

Sherman, Robert B, Bruce Gordon, Jeff Kurtti, and Richard M Sherman. *Walt's Time: From Before to Beyond*. Edited by David Mumford. Santa Clarita, CA: Camphor Tree Publishers, 1998.

Sherman, Robert B. Moose. Bloomington, IN: Authorhouse, 2013.

Sklar, Marty J., Ray Bradbury, and Richard M Sherman. *Dream It! Do It! (the People, the Places, the Projects): My Half-Century Creating Disney's Magic Kingdoms*. New York: Disney Publishing Worldwide, 2013.

Taves, Isabella and Lillian Disney. "I Live with a Genius." *McCall's* February 1953: 38–107.

Titizian, Joseph. "Recap: Our Grandpa, Walt Disney." October 9, 2015. Accessed August 28, 2016. http://www.waltdisney.org/blog/recap-our-grandpa-walt-disney.

Walt Disney Family Museum; various exhibits 2015 and 2016.

Walt Disney Productions. *Independent-Press-Telegram*. n.p., 1955.

Wilck, Tommie. (1968) Walt Disney Archives Interview.

Working with Walt: Interviews with Disney Artists. Jackson: University Press of Mississippi, 2008.

ACHNOWLEDGMENTS

My first readers and cheerleaders: Imagineers Tom Fitzgerald and Kathy Mangum. John Lasseter, for championing my project along with his team of dynamos—Heather Feng, Michele Moretta, and Tanya Oskansian.

Walt's family: Jenny Miller Goff, Tamara Miller, and Ron Miller. The Walt Disney Family Museum, for sharing precious images from their collection.

My Main Street, U.S.A. windows—Disney Legends all: Jim Cora (also my top intern), Marty Sklar, Bob Gurr, Tony Baxter, and Ron Dominguez.

My editor, Wendy Lefkon, for her commitment to flying this kite together, plus her deft editing, shared enthusiasm, and cheerful guidance. My agent, Steve Troha, who pushed me until I found *The Kingdom of Good Eating* and Folio Literary Management.

Book designer Iain R. Morris, who, with his own version of pixie dust, created a stunning mid-century time capsule, and Cameron + Company.

The Disney Dream Team: I am indebted to the Walt Disney Archives. Research has never been this much fun (or more thorough). Director Becky Cline and archivists Kevin M. Kern and Ed Ovalle (and their cheerful assistant Alesha Reyes). And for his sage consultation, Disney Legend and Chief Archivist Emeritus Dave Smith. Michael Buckhoff, in the Walt Disney Photo Archives, who always responded with the speed of a high-speed shutter. Thanks as well to Diane Scoglio, Aileen Kutaka, and David Stern at Walt Disney Imagineering, with a special shout-out to Vanessa Hunt, who dug deep into the Walt Disney Imagineering Art Library to find hidden treasures. At Disney Editions, editors Jennifer Eastwood and Laura Hopper, managing editor Monica Vasquez, and production director Marybeth Tregarthen deserve much thanks. And copy editors Jennifer Black, Warren Meislin, and Mariel Pinciotti are proof positive that there can never be too many cooks in the book kitchen.

At Disneyland: my offices—where I wrote for my audience, with my audience at, on, or in Main Street, U.S.A.; Disneyland and Santa Fe Railroad; Plaza Inn; River Belle Terrace; Mark Twain Riverboat; Fantasyland's Casey Jr. patio; and the Tomorrowland Terrace. Also to Cast Members Mary Nivens, Kevin Rafferty Jr., Betsy Sanchez, Karlos Siqueiros, Steve Valkenberg, and Oscar.

Thank you to recipe testers Johanna Lasseter-Curtis, baker extraordinaire, and Maxine Bloom, one of the best cooks I know. And Ron and David DeFore, for perfecting and sharing their Silver Banjo Barbecue Sauce recipe.

Others I need to thank are Disney publicist MaryAnn Zissimos, Ruthie Tompson, Angie Bliss, Karen Paik, Lin Fornio, Jeff Kurtti, and Michael Broggie. Mike and Janeen Van Eaton and the Van Eaton Gallery. Nancy Hopkins, Vivian Santangelo of *Better Homes & Gardens*, and Meredith Corporation. Elizabeth and Lisa at Smoke Tree Ranch. The Richard Nixon Presidential Library and Museum. And Acre Coffee and Franchettis' in Santa Rosa, California, for letting me linger for hours while I was writing and never asking me to leave, even when they were closing.

More gratitude to Dr. Joann Hawk, Dr. Josephine Smith, Shelley Fitzsimmons, Cynthia Lester, Carole Shorentein Hays and Andrew Konigsberg, for taking care of my mind, body, soul, and spirit. Austin Bellach, for his mad iPhone photography skills. My Mozzarellas, for their support and encouragement.

I'd be remiss if I didn't thank artist and Disney Legend Herb Ryman, whom I never met but whose words guided me along the way: "It is for people like yourself to have the privilege and the duty of presenting Walt as a human being and a person who can be known, a person you can be close to."

Last and not least, my son, Bo, a fellow writer and a fine human being, and my daughter, Riley Rose, my favorite person to play in the park with, who aptly said in her sixth-grade essay, "My mom REALLY loves Disney! She's a total Disney geek!"

{ABOVE} *Plaza Inn interior concept art by Dorothea Redmond, 1965*

The following are some of the trademarks, registered marks, and service marks owned by Disney Enterprises, Inc.: *Adventureland*® Area; *Disney*®; *Disneyland*®; *Disneyland*® Park; *Disneyland*® Resort; *Fantasyland*® Area; *Frontierland*® Area; Imagineering; Imagineers; *Magic Kingdom*® Park; *Main Street, U.S.A.*® Area; *Tomorrowland*® Area; and *Walt Disney World*® Resort.

For more information address Disney Editions,
1101 Flower Street, Glendale, California 91201.
Editorial Director: *Wendy Lefkon*
Designed by *Iain R. Morris*

This book's producers would also like to thank Agnes Chu, Becky Cline, Betsy Singer, Chip Poakeart, Chris Taylor, Debra Kohls, Denise Brown, Fanny Sheffield, Frank Reifsnyder, Jennifer Black, Jennifer Grant, Jess Allen, Dave Stern, Kevin Lively, Kiran Jeffery, Kristin Rodack, MaryAnn Zissimos, Marybeth Tregarthen, Megan Grainger, Mike Jusko, Michael Serrian, Monica Vasquez, Monique Diman, Robert Oelslager, Rudy Zamora, Scott Piehl, Terry Downes, Tim Retzlaff, Vanessa Hunt, Warren Meislin, Mariel Pinciotti, and Winnie Ho.

ISBN 978-1-4847-8229-3 • FAC-029191-17153

Printed in Malaysia • Reinforced binding

First Hardcover Edition, September 2017 • 10 9 8 7 6 5 4 3 2 1

Visit www.disneybooks.com